Praise for Alan Ryan's *On Politics*

"Ryan's book is a magnificent piece of work, clear . . . and engaging. . . . [T]he reader is wonderfully caught up in an uninterrupted trajectory of thought. . . . [A]nyone remotely interested in political theory will profit from reading or dipping into Ryan's *On Politics*. . . . The amazing thing about Alan Ryan is that he has assembled so much of this in a single place, so accessible in this two-volume reservoir of historical and political knowledge. . . . It's a remarkable experience."

—Jeremy Waldron, *New York Review of Books*

"Epic. . . . *On Politics* comes crammed with smart observations and wise advice. Readers unfamiliar with figures such as Machiavelli, Montaigne, Montesquieu and Marsilius of Padua, or with scores of lesser-known political writers, will profit from its clear explanations and well-crafted prose."   —John Keane, *Financial Times*

"Remarkably detailed yet highly readable. . . . [C]ontemporary American politics lurk in the background, as Ryan, in this absorbing and edifying read, regularly reminds us of what modern citizens might gain from a deeper understanding of the roots of today's political ideals and loyalties." —*Publishers Weekly*, starred review

ON AUGUSTINE

ABOUT THE SERIES

In *On Politics*, Alan Ryan distilled nearly a half century's career of teaching political theory into a two-volume history of Western political thought that spans three thousand years of history from ancient Greece to the present. Each volume pairs Ryan's trenchant analysis with a biography of a major philosopher, a timeline of their life, as well as key excerpts from their most essential works.

The series includes: *On Aristotle*, *On Machiavelli*, *On Tocqueville*, *On Marx*, *On Augustine*, and *On Hobbes*.

ALSO BY ALAN RYAN

On Hobbes: Escaping the War of All Against All

On Marx: Revolutionary and Utopian

On Tocqueville: Democracy and America

On Machiavelli: The Search for Glory

On Aristotle: Saving Politics from Philosophy

On Politics: A History of Political Thought: From Herodotus to the Present

Liberal Anxieties and Liberal Education

John Dewey and the High Tide of American Liberalism

Bertrand Russell: A Political Life

Property

Property and Political Theory

J. S. Mill

The Philosophy of the Social Sciences

The Philosophy of John Stuart Mill

ON AUGUSTINE

The Two Cities

ALAN RYAN

LIVERIGHT PUBLISHING CORPORATION

A Division of W. W. Norton & Company
Independent Publishers Since 1923
New York / London

For information about permission to reproduce selections from this book, write to Permissions, Liveright Publishing Corporation, a division of W. W. Norton & Company, Inc., 500 Fifth Avenue, New York, NY 10110

For information about special discounts for bulk purchases, please contact W. W. Norton Special Sales at specialsales@wwnorton.com or 800-233-4830

Manufacturing by RR Donnelley Westford
Book design by Ellen Cipriano
Production manager: Anna Oler

ISBN 978-0-87140-707-8 (pbk.)

Liveright Publishing Corporation
500 Fifth Avenue, New York, N.Y. 10110
www.wwnorton.com

W. W. Norton & Company Ltd.
Castle House, 75/76 Wells Street, London W1T 3QT

1 2 3 4 5 6 7 8 9 0

CONTENTS

PREFACE

In the introduction to *On Politics*, I suggested that one measure of the book's success would be the readers who went and read the works of the authors I discussed. Some readers suggested that I might encourage them to do so by taking chapters of *On Politics* and adding to them substantial extracts from the works I hoped they would read. What follows is exactly that, with a short introduction to provide some of the context that the chapter's original placement in *On Politics* would have provided. As before, I am grateful to Bob Weil and William Menaker at Liveright, as well as to the Norton production team, for their help in making an author's life as easy as it can plausibly be made.

CHRONOLOGY

387	Is baptized by Saint Ambrose
388	Returns to Thagaste, establishes contemplative community
391	Is ordained priest at Hippo; Emperor Theodosius finally prohibits pagan worship
396	Becomes bishop of Hippo
397–400	Writes *Confessions*
402	Imperial capital is moved to Ravenna
410	Sack of Rome by Alaric's Visigoths
413–26	Writes *City of God*
430	Dies at Hippo, with city under siege by Visigoths
476	Conventional dating of end of western Roman Empire, with deposition of Romulus Augustus

INTRODUCTION

IN THE LONGER WORK from which the discussion of Augustine's two cities is drawn, Augustine faces in two directions. Writing in the declining days of the Roman Empire, he is a political thinker of late classical antiquity and, more importantly, a Latin father of the church, a theologian whose views are a major part of Christian thought, both in the Middle Ages and down to our own time. His impact on Christian theology was overwhelming, and it was that that gave weight to his understanding of politics. *On Politics* set out to do some justice to both aspects of Augustine, a task made easier in the context of a long book with discussions of Greek and Roman thinkers from Plato and Aristotle to Polybius and Cicero before, and discussions of Aquinas, Machiavelli, and Luther after. Here I provide an abbreviated version of that scene setting.

Augustine was above all else a Christian, and a passionate and indefatigable defender of his faith. This
means that his political thinking is always framed in
terms of the attitude that a devout Christian should
take toward the political order, indeed the social order
more generally, and God's creation most generally. Even
more important than what a Christian does in the
political realm is his attitude toward what he does. *The
City of God* is not a work of political theory but, as it
says, a defense of Christianity "against the pagans." A
substantial part of the enormous work is ad hominem
in the sense that it is a defense of Christianity against
the charge of undermining the Roman Empire and so
bearing responsibility for the sack of Rome by Alaric
and the Visigoths in 410 CE. The simplest argument in
Augustine's armory is compelling, but essentially *tu quo-
que*: the pagan gods never protected their worshippers, at
Rome or elsewhere. However, Augustine engaged with
innumerable other topics, from the nature of original
sin to the origin of the world in space and time, Old
Testament chronology, the life spans of the patriarchs,
and very much else. Nonetheless, we might most readily
mark the contrast between Augustine's approach to
politics and that of his classical predecessors on the one
side and Machiavelli among others on the other side by
contrasting their this-worldly conception of political
success and his contempt for it. He repudiates the

search for glory, denies that a pagan city can practice true justice, and denies that self-sufficiency, whether individual or collective, is a possibility here on earth. The earthly political community should seek peace, suppress the lust for power, the *libido dominandi* that drove Rome, and try to secure the very limited kind of justice that a state can achieve. It was a realm in which our love of earthly goods could be harnessed to control the temptations presented by those same loves, as when we threaten punishment to deter theft or assault. Christians were obliged to obey the powers that be; as Saint Paul had said, the powers that be are ordained of God. Beyond that, their care should be for their eternal salvation, compared with which the vicissitudes of this life were insignificant.

Augustine's path to conversion (strictly speaking *re*conversion, since he had been brought up as a Christian before turning to Manichaeanism and Neoplatonism as a young man) was neither quick nor straightforward; but once he had been baptized, he abandoned the career as an imperial administrator that was the natural next step for someone with the talent that had taken him to a professorship of rhetoric in the imperial capital of Milan. Hoping to lead a secluded life in a small community of Christian contemplatives, he reluctantly accepted the call to serve the church, first as a priest and then as bishop of Hippo, the North

African town near his birthplace of Thagaste. Hippo
was a provincial capital in the Roman Empire, and is
today a substantial city in Algeria. As a bishop, Augustine played a practical role in secular matters as well as
in religious ones; he was called on to settle disputes
over property, hear complaints about assaults, and
manage the affairs of his congregation in matters both
secular and spiritual. The modern idea of a separation
of church and state was unknown in the ancient world.
This meant not only that a bishop performed secular
administrative tasks but that one of the tasks of a
Christian emperor was to protect the church, materi-
ally and spiritually. Augustine brought his own, distinctively Christian sensibilities to the task of settling
disputes within his own diocese and elsewhere, but he
never challenged the idea that the Christian faith, properly understood, should be promoted by the secular
authorities and, conversely, that the church should concern itself with the spiritual welfare of the emperor.
Once Christianity was the official religion of the
Roman Empire, as it had been since Constantine's conversion in 312, and more emphatically since the out-
lawing of pagan rituals and the destruction of pagan
temples between 380 and 391 under the emperor Theodosius, doctrinal uniformity was enforced in the last
resort by the criminal law.

Charity toward the misguided, and the not irredeemably wicked, was enjoined by the teaching of the church; but the modern notion of toleration lay many centuries in the future. Such toleration as was practiced in the ancient world, whether toward Christians by pagan officials or thereafter toward dissident Christians and pagans, was generally a matter of local officials' using their discretion to enforce the law with a light touch rather than a heavy hand; emperors, too, were often more concerned to keep the peace than to enforce doctrinal agreement. Both intellectually and morally speaking, there is a great difference between the tolerance that springs from an unreflectively relaxed attitude toward differences of opinion about religious matters, and the modern view, by no means universally accepted even in the secular Western world, and very much a minority view elsewhere, that however strong our disapproval of the religious views of other people, they have a right to hold them and express them, and it is not they who must keep quiet but we who must restrain our urge to silence them. The pre-Christian world was often— by no means always and everywhere—relaxed about the diversity of religious belief and practice, but it nowhere subscribed to principled toleration in the modern sense. Religious practice was important for social and political reasons, to create social solidarity, to court the favor of the gods, to underpin the local morality. Refusal to engage in the local ritual practices might well be treated as treason, therefore, but because it was not a theological issue, would not be punished as heresy even if it might be condemned as blasphemy.

The Christian concept of heresy was something of a novelty. Socrates was sentenced to death for introducing novel gods, for blasphemy and corrupting the young, but not for heresy. "Blasphemy" was a matter of insulting the gods, or denying their existence. Socrates did not do so, although he, or Plato speaking for him, did insist that the traditional tales about them could not be true: the gods were depicted as adulterers and prone to greed, envy, anger, and other vices. Corrupting the young was perhaps the crucial charge. It is likely that the provocation for the charge was less Socrates's beliefs than the fact that he had been a close friend of Critias and Charmides, who were relatives of Plato, and two of the leaders of the oligarchy that briefly and brutally governed Athens in 404 BCE, after its defeat at the end of the Peloponnesian War, and perhaps because of his friendship with Alcibiades, who had betrayed the Athenians more than once. In much the same way, two millennia later, Thomas Hobbes was accused of corrupting the upper-class young men at the court of Charles II by his "atheism." But Hobbes was accused of heresy as well; he certainly held heterodox views on such issues as the nature of the Trinity and the authorship of the so-called Mosaic books of the Old Testament. The Greek and Roman condemnation of blasphemy, or insulting the gods, or introducing new gods, reflected a desire to protect a traditional order. The devotions of the citizens were affirmations of an attachment to the mores of the city. They also kept the gods favorable to the city that honored them. There was a contractual element: the gods would resent any failure by a city to do them honor, and the gods laid themselves open to reproach if they failed to protect the city that honored them. That is why Augustine's most often repeated blow "against the pagans" in *The City of God* is the reminder that the pagan gods had done nothing to prevent the sack of 410.

The civic religions of Greece and Rome were backed by myths, but had no philosophical depth. The literary, anthropological, or psychological analysis of myths is another matter, and can be pursued at great depth, but the myths themselves did not provoke the philosophical analysis that the doctrine of the Trinity has prompted over the centuries. Zeus's turning himself into the swan that seduces Leda is of no theological interest. The Judaism that begat Christianity was very different from the civic cults of Greek and Roman cities inasmuch as they were polytheistic, and it was fiercely monotheistic. But Christianity was different again. Judaism was committed to the fastidious observance of divine law, but that resulted in the elaboration of a legal code, not a systematic theology. As a historical religion, Judaism was built around the story of God's dealings with his chosen people, and even more than the civic religions of classical city-states, it implied a covenant between God and his chosen people, but not one that gave the people any entitlement to complain about God's misbehavior. Unlike Christianity, Judaism was a non-proselytizing religion, but the insistence of the Jewish God that his people should have no other God but him meant that Jews, like Christians after them, could not worship strange gods, including deified Roman emperors, and for that they were persecuted as Christians were. Christianity, however, was both universal in the offer of redemption and replete with philosophical difficulties. How Christ could be at once fully divine and fully human was the central issue, and arguments over the nature of the Trinity have not ceased to this day. If Saint Paul had never been born, it is anyone's guess what Christianity might have become. What it did become was a religion committed to doctrinal orthodoxy, and in both the Latin West and the Greek East, the church relied on the secular authorities to repress heresy. The task of calling councils of the church to settle disputes, both credal and other, fell to the imperial authorities, even to the emperor himself.

Augustine's reflections on politics exist in two distinct forms. In *The City of God*, which alone is discussed here, he grapples with the largest questions that confront anyone given to reflection on politics, Christian or not, as well as those that Christians in particular must confront; what does our duty to obey our rulers rest on, what justifies punishment, may Christians serve in the armed forces or as agents of the system of criminal justice, even perhaps as executioners? What in the last resort is the purpose of earthly government? If it is not the pursuit of glory, as both Polybius long before and Machiavelli long afterward took it for granted that it is, then what is it? *The City of God* provides an answer, essentially that government protects earthly peace, the goods of this world, and secures a "sort of" justice, though not the true justice that God alone can institute. But Augustine also engaged in a continuous, very lengthy correspondence with Roman officials, members of his own and other congregations, fellow bishops, scholars, and others. Anyone concerned to know what Christian political practice amounted to for Augustine can trace it out in these letters in a way they cannot do in *The City of God*, even reading imaginatively between the lines. Much of Augustine's time as a bishop was taken up with the so-called Donatists, followers of Donatus, an unorthodox Christian leader from the early fourth century, who had taken a particularly intransigent line during the last of the Roman persecutions; Christians had been required to surrender their gospels, sacred vessels, and everything else required for Christian religious services. The imperial authorities would then destroy them. Those who refused faced execution. Donatus and his followers insisted that they must refuse. Those who were too frightened or who thought that it must be permissible to hand over mere physical objects were labeled *traditores*, "handers-over," a term that is the origin of the word "traitor." The Catholic Church in Africa was plagued by the Donatists for many years; they refused to accept the authority of the church when they were declared heretical, would not acknowledge the authority of bishops chosen by anyone whom they regarded as *traditores*, or as insufficiently hostile to the *traditores*, denied the efficacy of the sacraments performed by priests whose authority they did not accept, and resorted to violence in driving priests out of their churches. In fending them off, Augustine enunciated a principle that is highly persuasive in itself, but that was pregnant with trouble in the very distant future. The Donatists held that sacraments performed by a priest who—in their view—was unfit for the priesthood were inefficacious. Baptism, marriage, the mass, and the last rites would fail of their aim. Augustine's response was that it was the office, not the man, that mattered; and it was the sacrament, not the officiant, that counted. In the hands of Luther and other Protestant thinkers, this became the doctrine of the priesthood of all believers and made it hard to see why an institutional church was necessary at all.

The largest political questions were not raised by the daily necessity of keeping the peace among squabbling congregants, advising younger bishops on the need for tact in dealing with their flock, and so generally on. The largest issues arose in the context of the continued, though increasingly fragile, existence of the western Roman Empire; and the intellectual apparatus that Augustine brought to them was both Christian and classical. Before his return to the Christian faith, Augustine had been influenced by the Neoplatonic philosophy of Plotinus, although he may not have read Plato at first hand. His entry point into philosophy had been Cicero, who was notably eclectic, both by temperament and as a matter of pedagogy, and especially because of what he conceived the place of philosophy in public life to be. It was to provide the arguments that illuminated and sustained the virtues that a properly brought-up Roman of the upper classes would have been taught to practice. This was not the sum total of what philosophy did; it provided consolations for the misfortunes inevitable in human life, and illuminated our relations with the universe and eternity. Its public role was more practical and pragmatic; Cicero thought that skilled oratory was the highest mental acquisition because it enabled a man to play a proper part in public life. Plato, however, had condemned rhetoric as a skill like that of pastry cooks and prostitutes, agreeable for the consumer but bad for their health and morals. Augustine was closer to Plato and did not accept Cicero's view that we should say what was appropriate to the audience we were attempting to persuade. Augustine was an astonishingly gifted writer, and his success as a teacher of rhetoric is easy to understand, but he was committed to pursuing the truth, however painful and unpalatable. Augustine was in that respect a true disciple of Plato, and it made him a formidable theologian whose authority was rivaled only by that of Aquinas almost nine centuries later. None of that made him susceptible to Plato's utopian visions, or to Aristotle's claim that the polis was the highest form of community. As Saint Paul said in his Epistle to the Hebrews, we have here no lasting city; our real home is the city of God.

Augustine could not wholeheartedly follow the classical philosophers in their search for self-sufficiency, either individual or political. He wrestled with the doctrine of original sin in all manner of contexts, and had a host of interesting things to say about it, but a crucial aspect of the doctrine for his view of the political condition is that it rules out earthly self-sufficiency as the goal of philosophical understanding. We are wholly dependent on the mercy of God, and that fact should inform our every waking thought. We should try to live a tranquil existence to the extent the world permits it, but in the last resort it is not we but God who will decide our fate. The political implications of such a worldview are what the discussion of Augustine in *On Politics* is concerned with. Here we may briefly focus on how sharp a break it makes with classical political ideals. Aristotle treated the Greek polis as the proper environment for the practice of politics because it was self-sufficient, unlike the family or the village, which required the protection of the polis to guarantee their continued existence. Man, as Aristotle remarked, is an animal intended by nature to live in a polis, or, more briefly, man is a political animal. By no means all men, and no women at all, are fitted for political life, however. Only well-educated, reasonably well-off men were fit to be citizens; economic self-sufficiency is important because a man who must spend all his time laboring has no leisure to think intelligently about politics. Moreover, geography matters as well; too hot or too bleak a climate leaves men unable to focus their attention on governing themselves. Unsurprisingly, Greece was the natural home of political life. Pauline Christianity looked to an afterlife in which there was neither Jew nor Gentile, slave nor free. Quibbling about this-worldly constitutional arrangements was beside the point.

Treating constitutional arrangements as neither here nor there marked a radical break with a long tradition, and one that reasserted itself almost a millennium after Augustine. Aristotle appealed to "what men say" about the virtues of citizens and the best kind of constitution, and although he was aristocratic in his allegiances, he is probably a good guide to what educated Greeks of the fifth and fourth centuries BCE thought about politics. One thing that he reports many men as saying is that the best constitution is the mixed constitution that blends monarchy, aristocracy, and democracy to secure the benefits of each of the simple forms of constitution and offset their weaknesses. The model was the Spartan constitution, a byword for stability; its successor in the literature of constitutional construction was the Roman Republic as praised by Polybius and Cicero. The monarchical element was supplied by the consuls, the aristocratic element by the senate, and the democratic element by the people at large in electing officials and ratifying laws. Its modern successor is the constitution of the United States, generally described as a liberal democracy, but understood by its creators as a mixed republic. The Athenians, whose constitutional arrangements Aristotle, or his students, described in detail, were unusual in their attachment to democracy. They saw it as an expression of their determination to have no master. They had experienced tyranny under the Peisistratids during the latter half of the sixth century BCE, they thought of Sparta as brutal and oligarchical, and they wished to be self-governing in the most literal sense. Athenian democracy was direct democracy; citizens attended the assembly in person, listened to debates, and voted. They also served in the law courts, where they were both judge and jury; and in important cases, such as Socrates's trial for insulting the gods and corrupting the young, the jury had 501 members, something like one in forty of all citizens eligible to serve. Conviction and sentencing were by majority vote. The Athenians thought they were uniquely free in being self-governing in such a fashion. But Romans, too, thought their form of government achieved freedom. Rome, like all ancient city-states, relied very heavily on slaves; in Roman law the crucial contrast was between a slave and a free citizen; our concept of "liberty" stems from the Latin *liber*, which described someone who was his own master, from which much else flowed. There was also a long Roman tradition that held that a state ruled by a "king"—one absolute ruler—had to all intents and purposes reduced everyone to the condition of a slave. So committed were the Romans to this view that an emperor was *imperator*, not *rex*. He was a commander, not a king. A republican constitution provided stability and liberty, and sustained a free government. This was the idiom of Americans revolting against the monarchical rule of George III, and whatever the justice of the charge that he was a tyrant, the charge itself belonged to a very ancient tradition of political argument.

It was to preserve the republican constitution of Rome that Caesar's assassins murdered him; the Roman constitution provided for temporary dictatorship to deal with emergencies, almost always military. In the last century of the republic's life, a sequence of warlords had themselves appointed dictator for longer, sometimes indefinite, periods. The history of the empire that came into existence soon afterward is not our subject. What is more germane is that with the establishment of autocracy, Rome adopted many of the practices that had long characterized the monarchies of the eastern Mediterranean and the Near East. The most striking of these was the conferring of divinity upon the emperor and the creation of an attendant imperial cult. Until Christianity became the official religion of the Roman Empire, the most likely cause of conflict between Christians and the imperial authorities was a refusal to sacrifice to the emperor. Such a refusal was treason. Sacrificing was like reciting the Pledge of Allegiance in an American school; those who refuse are making a point about their dislike of the government of the day. Henry VIII's former chancellor, Sir Thomas More, was executed in 1535 because he would not acknowledge Henry as the supreme head of the Church of England; fealty to the pope was not a permissible difference of opinion about the best mode of church government, but treason. Once the Roman Empire became Christian, the imperial cult was abandoned.

Augustine broke with the classical tradition in almost ignoring the question of which regimes are best, and in setting his face against the common assumption that the pursuit of glory was the proper aim of a state. The Athenians who would have no master prided themselves on their dominance of the Aegean; Pericles did not scruple to say that their rule over their notional allies in the Delian League was all but "tyrannical." Their allies' contribution to the common funds of the league built the Parthenon and beautified Athens; the allies received protection from the formidable Athenian navy, but the bargain was very much one struck in favor of Athens. The same story could be told even more emphatically about Rome. Certainly, there was always an undertone of anxiety in the self-praise of Athenian or Roman orators; boasting might attract the malevolent attention of the fates. Whether Rome could really expect to be the eternal city, when so many previous empires had risen and fallen, many of them destroyed by Roman expansion, was a question often asked sotto voce. Augustine's target in *The City of God* is the Roman historian Varro (116–27 BCE), who survived the collapse of the republic and wrote a celebratory history of the rise and greatness of Rome. Augustine's view was

that what Rome thought of as glory was the gratification of a desire we should try to suppress: the *libido dominandi*, or a lust to lord it over others.

Like other writers in the Christian tradition, Augustine leaned heavily on Saint Paul's injunction to "obey the
powers that be." The question of the sense in which any
particular ruler is "ordained of God" is not at stake; more
than a millennium later, defenders of divine right monarchy had to answer that question, but Augustine did not.
What was ordained of God was the existence of rulers.
Neither their pedigree, their competence, nor their moral
character was for their subjects to scrutinize. Here was
another decisive break with the classical tradition in
which tyrannicides were praised as the saviors of the
republic. On Augustine's view, the tyrant was as likely as
not to be a justified punishment for our misdeeds. The
duty of obedience was absolute in everything that did not
require the Christian subject to act against his faith. By
the same token, that included the faithful performance of
whatever civic duties we might be required to perform,
whether it was serving as a soldier—in a just war—or in
keeping the peace, serving as a judge, even as an executioner, although Augustine was opposed to capital
punishment, as he was to torture. Punishment should
aim at reformation, and a dead man is beyond reform;
as for torture, a man might confess to almost anything
to spare himself its pains, meaning that he added the

sin of lying to whatever crime he might or might not have committed, while a judge ran the risk that he would be guilty of the much worse sin of punishing the innocent.

A thumbnail sketch of the political systems that emerged in the Latin West after the collapse of the western Roman Empire soon after Augustine's death, in 430 CE, would serve little purpose. New states eventually crystallized out of the barbarian kingdoms, many of them monarchies, others city republics, all of them at least notionally Christian and owing fealty to the pope. They did not practice Augustinian politics in any distinctive fashion. The doctrine that "the powers that be are ordained of God" was Pauline rather than Augustinian, although Augustine himself firmly believed in it. The doctrine in any case left a good deal of room for argument over the legitimacy of any particular ruler, and Augustine's insistence that any government that preserved earthly peace was as acceptable as any other did not provide the resources for deciding between rival candidates for earthly power. The most intense medieval struggles were between church and state; ideologically, they hinged on interpretations of the doctrine of the two swords put forward sixty years after Augustine's death by Pope Gelasius I. In 494 CE Gelasius told the emperor Anastasius that there were two distinct powers conferred by Christ, the secular embodied in the emperor and the spiritual embodied in the pope. The second was "weightier" because the pope was charged to care for the spiritual health of all Christians, the emperor included. In the Greek-speaking eastern empire, which survived until 1453 and the fall of Constantinople, this became a dead letter, and the emperor continued to appoint the patriarch of Constantinople and to convene councils of the church; in the West, the papacy struggled to secure the right of the college of cardinals to elect the pope without lay interference, and eventually succeeded. Following the creation of the Holy Roman Empire—"neither Holy, nor Roman, nor an Empire," as was often remarked—first with the coronation of Charlemagne in 800 CE and more lastingly that of Otto I in 962, the stage was set for centuries of conflict between the empire and papacy for supremacy in Italy; the emperor of the day was crowned by the pope, and the pope depended on imperial military power, so either might reasonably have claimed that the authority of the other depended on his own good grace. The beneficiaries of the stalemate that usually obtained were the Italian city-states that wished to be subservient to neither party.

To none of these struggles were Augustine's views especially relevant. His direct impact was greater in a nonpolitical sphere, the regulation of monastic life, where later reformers, Saint Benedict among them, built

on the rules Augustine laid down for the community at
Hippo. Some of his subsequent impact was mediated
through Martin Luther and the success of the Protestant Reformation. Luther's views on the inadmissibility
of rebellion, his insistence that a good Christian must
be ready to serve as a soldier, even as an executioner, as
well as much of his theology, were thoroughly Augustinian. In the twentieth century Augustine's impact was
felt, perhaps in an exaggerated form, in discussions of
the "just war." Augustine certainly had a doctrine of
the just war; more clearly than anyone before him, he
distinguished between the *ius ad bellum* and the *ius in
bello*, between just grounds for making war at all and
just methods of fighting. It is not clear that he was
original in his views; Cicero certainly held much the
same view of what justice with regard to warfare
involved, and Augustine writes as though it was a
common view among other thinkers in the church.
Original or not, Augustine's views became important
to twentieth-century Christian pacifists and others
who hoped to see moral constraints on the conduct of
war. Perhaps the most interesting impact of Augustine
in the past few decades has been his chastening effect
on liberal thinkers. Whatever cause one might recruit
Augustine for, it was not mindless cheerfulness and
unbridled optimism about human progress. Indeed,
Reinhold Niebuhr, who reminded his fellow radicals to

take the reality of original sin seriously, complained mildly that Augustine underestimated the possibilities of a meliorist social and political regime. But Niebuhr's famous essay *The Children of Light and the Children of Darkness*, written in the early post–World War II years, caught the authentic note. Certainly totalitarians of a Nazi or Stalinist persuasion were children of darkness and must be struggled against; but we should not deceive ourselves about our own purity. Niebuhr had an enormous impact on a generation of scholars who not only gave mid-twentieth-century American liberalism its distinctive tone of voice but also served American governments as advisers, as administrators, and sometimes as ambassadors. It is easy to imagine that a chastened determination to make the best of our time as "pilgrims" here on earth is what a modern-day Augustine would urge on us. Our earthly loves may not make us citizens of the city of God, but they are not to be despised as guides to our conduct while we are here as citizens of the earthly city.

ON AUGUSTINE

Augustine: The Two Cities

AUGUSTINE'S LIFE AND TIMES

A UGUSTINE'S IMPORTANCE TO THE subsequent history of Europe is impossible to exaggerate. His political theory, which is all we focus on here, was a very small part of what he wrote in some 113 books and innumerable letters and sermons. Nonetheless, it is pregnant with arguments that racked not only Christian Europe but the modern world: how seriously should a Christian with his eyes on eternity take the politics of this earthly life; is it the duty of the state to protect the church, repress heresy, and ensure that its citizens adhere to the one true faith; absent a Christian ruler, are we absolved of the duty to obey our rulers, or must we follow Saint Paul's injunction to "obey the powers that be"?[1] More generally, Augustine articulated distinctive and long-lived thoughts on matters that remain controversial: the nature of just war, the illegiti-

macy of the death penalty, the limits of earthly justice.
The fact that his views on all these matters were embed-
ded in a theology of some bleakness does not mean that
they do not survive on their own merits. One needs only
the barest sympathy with the thought that we are fallen
creatures to find many of his views deeply appealing, far
from cheerful as they may be.

Augustine was a Roman citizen, born at Thagaste,
in North Africa, in 354. It is generally assumed that he
was ethnically a Berber. His father was a minor official,
a decurion; the rank was initially a military rank in the
auxiliary forces with which Rome kept order in the
provinces; the civilian equivalent was a town manager.
The family's curial rank mattered less than that his
parents were just prosperous enough to send Augustine
to boarding school at the age of eleven. His mother,
Monica, was a devout but uneducated Christian, his
father a non-Christian who may or may not have converted on his deathbed. Catholic Christianity had
recently become the official religion of the Roman
Empire, the final great persecution of the Christians
having taken place under Diocletian in 305–6. Augustine was not baptized as a child, but infant baptism was
far from universal. He claimed that he had a wholly
miserable childhood. In *The City of God* he says that he
would rather die than live his childhood over again; but
the claim comes in one of his many descriptions of

human life as a long journey through a vale of suffering, and is not conclusive evidence that his childhood
was more miserable than most childhoods or than his
subsequent life. Indeed, he does not suggest that it was,
since he asks rhetorically, "If anyone were offered the
choice of suffering death or becoming a child again,
who would not recoil from the second alternative and
choose to die?"[2]

He claimed that as a child he disliked learning and
preferred the pain of punishment for refusing to learn
Greek to the pain of the lessons. He also says, perfectly
sensibly, that Latin came easily because everyone around
him spoke it, but Greek did not, because it was a foreign
language. Many of us have thought as much about the
languages we have tried to learn. He was certainly very
clever and perhaps as willful as he claimed; how much
Greek he learned is unclear, but it seems likely that he
could read it without great difficulty but much preferred
Latin. He initially intended to advance himself with a
career in the imperial administration. This required a
training in the skills of the orator, and at sixteen he
went to Carthage to learn rhetoric. While there, he took
a mistress by whom he had a son, Adeodatus. In retrospect, he was appalled by these youthful yieldings to the
urgings of the flesh. Modern readers of his *Confessions*
find them wholly forgivable and are much more appalled
that he never tells us the name of his mistress, and that

he abandoned her a dozen years later—as anyone of his class and upbringing would have done—when he was minded to marry an heiress to advance his career.[3]

He taught rhetoric in North Africa, then Rome, and when he was thirty secured a distinguished position as professor of rhetoric in Milan, which was a stepping-stone to a provincial governorship. By this time Rome was no longer the imperial capital. Early in the fourth century Diocletian had established his eastern capital at Byzantium and his western capital in Milan. Under Constantine the imperial capital was Byzantium, now renamed Constantinople, but late in the century the empire became de facto an eastern and western empire, with the western capital at Milan, and later at Ravenna. When teaching in Milan, Augustine arranged to make an advantageous marriage, essential to membership of the Roman aristocracy, but after much mental anguish he renounced these ambitions, was baptized as a Christian in 386, and devoted himself to the service of the church. He was baptized by Ambrose, bishop of Milan, the most intellectually and politically powerful churchman of his day, but it was devout lay friends who had done the work of conversion, or reconversion, since he had been brought up as a Christian as a child and had abandoned his faith in Carthage. He had by this time explored many of the religious and quasi-religious resources of the late classical world. He was for a time a

Manichaean "hearer" or acolyte, but found Manichaeanism intellectually unpersuasive and littered with
superstition and myth. He was then attracted by the
austere Neoplatonism of the pagan philosopher Plotinus, which was a very plausible gateway to the Christian
faith. Once he had become a Christian, he returned to
North Africa, first to Thagaste, where he set up a little
community of celibate Christians, and then to Hippo,
where he was inducted as a priest in 391 and made
bishop in 395, taking up office in 396. He spent the
second half of his life as bishop of Hippo, in continual
controversy with movements he thought heretical or
otherwise a danger to the church, and writing a stream
of books and pamphlets to defend his view of the true
church and the true faith.

One of the first things he wrote as bishop was a
book that defies categorization, the *Confessions*, written
in 397–400 and read with passionate interest ever since.
Although it is a record of the route by which he came to
his Christian faith, it is not an autobiography in the
modern, or even in the ancient, sense. It is more nearly a
continuous prayer to the God who had saved him,
accompanied by lengthy passages of self-recrimination
based loosely on his recollection of particular episodes
of wrongdoing. It is made unforgettable by Augustine's
extended reflections on the sheer mysteriousness of
human existence. The first ten books are a loosely

chronological *apologia pro vita sua*; the last three discuss time, the Trinity, and the Creation. Even readers who find Augustine's emotional style overpowering find it deeply engrossing, atheists as much as Christians.[4]

A bishop was not a grand figure in the church of the late fourth century. There were seven hundred bishops in the African church alone. He was nonetheless a central figure in the ordinary secular administration of his region, called on to exercise judicial functions and much else. Although such a life was not entirely thankless, it was exhausting, and Augustine lived it against the background of a steady decline in the western Roman Empire's ability to defend itself and protect its subjects. In 410 came the shattering event that launched Augustine on the task that occupied him for much of the rest of his life: writing *The City of God against the Pagans*, begun in 413 and completed after many interruptions in 427. When Alaric and his Visigoths sacked Rome in 410, the Eternal City was revealed as the indefensible former capital of the crumbling, and less important, western portion of the Roman Empire. The event was less important militarily than symbolically, but its symbolic importance was vast. Although Augustine does not mention it, Roman rule was decaying in North Africa as it was elsewhere. Roman control was increasingly fragile away from the coastal cities, and the military units meant to keep the peace on Rome's behalf were decreasingly under the control of the imperial administration, adding another danger to the incursions of barbarian tribes. In the last years of Augustine's life, the Vandals who had seized Spain realized that the province of Africa was at their mercy, and crossed the narrow straits to seize their prey. Augustine died in 430, with Hippo a besieged city full of refugees from the surrounding country. It was sacked and burned the following year.

In spite of the innumerable Renaissance paintings of Augustine at his desk, his daily round as a bishop was not spent in the study. He spent most mornings giving judgment in litigation over land, inheritances, and the other business of everyday life. His pastoral mission involved keeping his clergy even more than the laity on the straight and narrow, and managing intense relationships with the most spiritually aware of his congregation. Through his writings, Augustine would be second only to Saint Paul in his impact on the history of Christianity, but not only could he not have guessed this might happen; it would have been incredible to anyone else. The intellectual life of the Christian churches was still more Greek than Roman; Ambrose and Augustine were among the first Latin fathers, but that retrospective status was not something they set out to acquire. Greek was the language of philosophy, and Augustine's knowledge of Greek philosophy was sec-

ondhand, acquired from Cicero and from Latin transla-
tions of the Neoplatonist Plotinus. The churches of
Constantinople or Jerusalem would have seemed much
more likely sources of a Christian theology with real
intellectual power.

As a Roman of the western empire, Augustine was
not a natural intellectual leader of the Catholic Church.
As an African, he was a provincial; the African church
was provincial, too. It had a more austere view of the
demands of Christianity than did the church in Italy; it
did not accept the aristocratic laissez-faire that allowed
Roman families to be partly pagan and partly Christian
in their practice, and it was intolerant of doctrinal loose-
ness. Retrospectively, we can see Catholic doctrine crys-
tallizing into an orthodoxy; Augustine's contemporaries
would have thought it was an open question where Christianity would settle on issues such as the freedom of the
will, predestination, original sin, and the requirements
for salvation. Augustine's vast and unwieldy masterpiece,
The City of God, takes such firm and uncompromising
views on all these issues that we are not surprised they
triumphed; they have an unmatched intellectual power.
Yet the price—intellectual, emotional, and moral—that
must be paid for holding Augustine's views is so high that
it is equally surprising that they made any headway.

Augustine excoriated himself for ever holding his
pre-Christian beliefs. Nonetheless, they greatly influ-

enced his view of the world as a Christian. To say that he remained a Neoplatonist or a Manichee would be foolish; to say that in temperament and in intellectual style he remained the man who found Manichaeanism and Neoplatonism attractive is the bare truth. This was not only a matter of Augustine's temperament and intellect. Christian doctrine was much affected both by the mysticism of the oriental mystery religions and by the rationalism of Greek philosophy. We can find our way into, and perhaps out of, Augustine's *City of God* most readily if we start with the dilemmas that any devout Christian must face when contemplating earthly politics, wrestle first with Augustine's youthful opinions, and enter *The City of God* by way of his confrontation with Cicero's *De republica.* This will involve a perhaps surprising degree of attention to the doctrinal pressures on Augustine, but much as Plato thought that only the truth as he saw it could redeem earthly societies, so Augustine, who thought that nothing but the grace of God could redeem anything mortal, thought that the truth inherent in his Christian faith contained the key to the value, limited as it was, of our earthly politics, as well as the explanation of the chasm that separated those politics from the non-politics of the true kingdom of God. Where philosophers and theologians are convinced that their ideas stand or fall as a systematic whole, there is nothing for us to do but to explore the edifice they have constructed.

POLITICS AND RELIGION

Between the death of Cicero in 43 BCE and the birth of Augustine four centuries later, enormous changes had occurred. The most immediately momentous was the collapse of the Roman Republic and its gradual transformation into an empire. No thumbnail sketch of the following four centuries is possible here; but the crucial transformations can be briefly outlined. After the civil wars that followed the assassination of Julius Caesar, Caesar's adoptive grandson, Octavian, emerged victorious and established the "principate" that was recognized as the institution of one-man rule. The Roman hostility to the concept of a "king" remained as intense as ever, and for a surprisingly long time the forms of republican institutions were preserved. What we now think of as the imperial structure of administration and government was very late in coming. Only when the entire empire was threatened by military disasters and economic and administrative chaos during the third century was there a radical transformation of its political structure that kept the empire alive for another century in the west and another millennium in the east.

A succession of emperors who gained power by military prowess created the centralized, bureaucratic, and uniform system of administration that we think of as defining the imperial system. The empire's ambition to rule the known world remained, even if the western empire was increasingly a patchwork of local regimes whose subordination to the empire was a legal fiction. At a doctrinal level, the Roman ideology of consensus, honored in the breach as it had always been, yielded to an emphasis on obedience and order. In terms of the contrast we began with, citizens gave way to subjects, and as emperors were increasingly drawn from the eastern empire, a more "Persian" view of a ruler's status crystallized. Christian rulers could not receive divine honors, but their pagan predecessors did, and the elaborate ceremonial of the court at Constantinople under Christian emperors was scarcely different.

The transformation of the pagan empire into the Christian empire that Constantine began to create and that became solidly established when Theodosius, the last emperor to reign over both the eastern and the western empires, outlawed pagan cults late in the fourth century, was in the long run even more momentous. The Christianization of the regions and peoples that composed the Roman Empire survived the decay of the western empire and ensured that the "barbarian" kingdoms that succeeded the western empire were Christian societies, just as the Byzantine Empire was. Somewhat fortuitously the Christianization of barbarian Europe fostered the process by which the pope ceased to be one bishop among many and became the head of the entire western church. The only language of law and culture they possessed in common was Latin—the language of western but not Greek Christianity—and Latin thus became the universal language of Western culture and gave the western Catholic Church a distinct identity.

Until Pippin and Charlemagne established the kingdom of the Franks in the eighth century, the Catholic Church was the only institution whose authority aspired to the geographical reach of the western empire. This sustained the concept of the universality of Roman rule while spiritualizing it in a way republican Romans would have found strange. It need not have happened. In retrospect the preeminence of the pope as the heir of Saint Peter seems inevitable, but when Constantine made Christianity the religion of the empire, it was to his city that eyes turned rather than to Rome. Thereafter, Milan and Ravenna were as important as Rome. Looking back, we see the ingredients assembled for the creation of the distinctive institutions of church and state, cooperating but serving different ends, and always in danger of coming into conflict either over doctrine or over the privileges of the clergy or over the different loyalties they appealed to. But if the western and eastern halves of the Roman Empire had not gone their separate ways, the history of Christianity would have been very different, and our ideas about the naturalness of a division of labor between religious and secular institutions would have been very different, too.[5]

The theoretical analysis of the role of religion in politics or of the politics of religion in all its forms is made harder by the ambiguity of both concepts. Politics and religion resist simple definition; nor can we wish these ambiguities away. It is of the essence of both religion and politics that it is an open question what is and is not a religious consideration or a political one. Politics as a simple struggle for power is not politics as Aristotle conceived it—the citizens of a polis ruling and being ruled in turn; and the politics of a society that seeks to find a "godly ruler" is not like either. The boundaries of the concept of religion are so porous that we habitually distinguish between "organized religion" and a "religious" view of the world more generally, with many writers thinking the first an enemy of the second.[6] The crucial contrast for our immediate purposes is between Christian politics and pagan politics: between the political implications of a theologically complex, fiercely monotheistic Christianity and the political implications of the theologically casual, polytheistic, "civic" religions of the Greek and Roman world. The contrast sheds light on the difficulties that pagan rulers had with the unwillingness of Jews and Christians to sacrifice to the local deities and on the very thin sense in which their persecutions were "religious" in motivation, and it also illuminates the first and most important articulation of Christian political theology.[7]

The very idea of a Christian political theology is problematic. If human beings are only transitorily on earth, and earth is but a vale of tears through which we must pass on our way to paradise, earthly politics loses almost all value. Life in the polis cannot be the good life for man, since fulfillment lies in the hereafter; here below, we must prepare for eternity. Earthly happiness for rational persons consists in whatever confidence they may entertain about the life hereafter. This "abstentionist" vision is in some ways at odds with the involvement of Christ in the everyday life of the community in which he spent his short life. He may not have taken part in "politics," and he certainly insisted that his kingdom was "not of this world." But he healed the sick, preached to large crowds, and taught an ethical system that would have made a deep political impact on any society open to his teaching. Roman Judaea was not wholly deaf to it, which may well have been one reason for his execution. In the first two centuries after the death of Christ, Christianity might well have been thought un- or apolitical, however. The belief that Christ's return was imminent undermined a concern with earthly politics, and Christianity initially appealed mainly to the poor, to slaves, and to outsiders with no role in Roman political and public life. In the innumerable cities of the Greek east that preserved their earlier institutions by Roman concession, there was "local politics" still. There was also a great deal of public life both in the administration of justice and the provision of the usual services of government, and in semicompulsory public duties incumbent on the upper classes, such as laying on games and paying for sacrifices. As a religion of the poor, Christianity had nothing to offer public life.

Both in Rome and in the provinces, the civic life of the empire certainly impinged on Christians, however; they faced punishments up to and including hideous forms of death for refusing to sacrifice to the emperor of the day or to the Roman gods, and they might at any time be made scapegoats for a famine or some other misfortune. When persecutions became infrequent and when Christianity began to appeal to the higher social classes, who were bound to accept their share of public obligations, the question of how Christians should relate to the state became harder to evade. Finally, when the emperor Constantine converted to Christianity and the empire became Christian, all the questions so familiar to us about how the state should support religion, and how Christians should support a Christian or a non-Christian state, demanded answers. Christian thinkers had to form a view on vexed issues: how did God's law relate to civic law, and beyond that to the law of nature—*lex naturae*—and the law of peoples—the jus gentium? Could a Christian shed blood as a judge imposing the death penalty? Should Christians serve in an army? Early Christianity was overwhelmingly pacifist, but Constantine's Christianity was the reverse. What moral sacrifices, and how many, could a Christian make to be a good citizen? Augustine neither raised nor answered all these questions, but he provided the intellectual apparatus with which subsequent generations did.

MANICHAEANISM

The story is rich in paradox. Augustine was a fierce critic of pagan philosophy and adamant that only in Christianity could salvation be found; but he found his way to an intellectually cogent Christianity by way of Cicero's philosophical works and Neoplatonism. His conception of the two cities was foreshadowed in Scipio's Dream, with which Cicero's *De republica* concludes, just as Scipio's Dream was foreshadowed in Plato's contrast between the two realms in which the philosopher finds himself: the earthly republic and the reality revealed by philosophy. Initially, Augustine was tempted by Manichaeanism.

He began his search for faith as a Manichaean

"hearer," a spiritual fellow traveler who served the adepts of the faith—the illuminati—and prepared their food. Manichaeanism was not then the reviled heresy it became; there was no unified and authoritative source of Christian belief, such as the papacy became in medieval western Europe, and no authority able to impose a single view of orthodoxy and heresy. This did not encourage toleration, and it did not reflect a belief in the separateness of secular and spiritual authority; no premodern society entertained such a view. Churches and secular authorities repressed ideas they did not like, in a sporadic and inconsistent fashion; where they either could not do it or had no particular reason to do it, they were tolerant by accident rather than design. Manichaeanism was the creation of a third-century Persian sage, Mani, who described himself as the apostle of Christ.[8] Its one, very important intellectual strength was its answer to the problem of evil. The problem is simply stated: if God is both loving and omnipotent, why is there suffering in the world? Augustine eventually held that suffering exists because humanity is sinful, an answer built on an unflinching acceptance of the doctrine of original sin and the heritability of the taint of Adam. Pagan polytheisms did not face the problem. Evil was a brute fact, and accepted as such, unclouded by any idea that the gods might have intended there to be less of it.

Manichaeanism relied on one non-Christian—and non-Judaic—premise. It was dualistic. The material world is evil, as is all matter; that is why the world we live in is a realm of pain and suffering. The God revealed in the Old Testament is good, and is pure spirit; but contrary to Genesis, the physical world is not his creation but the work of the devil. For this reason, Manichaeanism held a negative view of sexual passion, both human and other. The created world is evil, as is our physical nature and sexual reproduction. This was one reason for the Manichaean commitment to vegetarianism, although the Manichaeanism of Augustine's day was independently committed to the virtues of fruits such as melons, which were identified with the sun, the supposed dwelling place of God. Sun worship was Zoroastrian, and the Zoroastrian element in Manichaeanism swiftly alienated Augustine. Mani's writings also made claims about stars and planets and phenomena such as eclipses that were patently false. When Augustine found that pagan writers had made careful celestial observations of eclipses and similar phenomena, and that their predictions were invariably right and Mani's wrong, his faith gave way.[9]

Nonetheless, the attractions of Manichaeanism are powerful. It does not blame innocent suffering on God. Innocent suffering is the rock on which Christianity is always in danger of shipwreck; critics of the Christian belief that this imperfect world is the creation of a benign omnipotence always point to the painful deaths of little children as clinching evidence that it cannot be. Either God is not omnipotent or he is not benign; few wish to bite the bullet and accept the third possibility— that tiny children are sinful and merit their suffering. Augustine bit the bullet, eventually arguing that we all enter the world tainted with the sin of Adam and deserve what we suffer.[10] One might think that the Manichaean view that God is the source of goodness, but unable to make headway against the devil, is less alarming. The persistence of Manichaeanism into the late Middle Ages suggests that many people have thought so.

Augustine's mother, the devout Monica, forbade Augustine the house while he was a hearer. Nonetheless, Manichees and Christians had a lot in common; and that was not surprising in an age when pagan philosophers numbered Christ among the wonder-workers and magi they admired, while rejecting as absurd the idea that a human could be literally the son of God, and dismissing the doctrine of the resurrection of the body as preposterous. Manichees saw Christ as the Gnostic heretics did: Christ was a great teacher. Like others who embodied great doctrines, he emanated from God, but was not literally his son. Nor could he have suffered bodily torment on the cross; the appearance that he did so was an illusion. Christ was pure spirit, and the human body that observers saw was the appearance that the divine spirit wore for temporary purposes. The point of Christ's mission was to spread enlightenment, and his work as a teacher was central to his life. The Resurrection was the emancipation of Christ's spirit from its earthly appearance, and resurrection for anyone else would similarly be the escape of the spirit from the body.

Gnostic sects were innumerable and various, and Manichaeanism embraced many local varieties, so it is impossible to give a more precise account of what Augustine believed than the one he gave in his *Confessions*. There are no competing accounts to set against his. The triumph of Christianity everywhere west of Persia and the dislike that political rulers felt for the anarchist implications of Manichaeanism mean that the literary remains of Manichaeanism are sparse. Precision is not necessary; once Christian orthodoxy embraced the Incarnation and the Resurrection of the body, Gnosticism was at odds with the two central items of the faith. The struggles internal to Christianity between Trinitarian and non-Trinitarian accounts of the divine nature were violent; but they were between Christians who shared precisely the doctrines that Manichees and Gnostics rejected.

Most religious faith owes less to its intellectual coherence, narrowly considered, than to two other elements. One is its ability to provide a lightning rod for powerful emotions; the other, the persuasiveness of the picture of the human condition it offers. For Augustine, Manichaeanism appealed to a powerful element in his character, his sense that he was full of bad desires. This was his personal "problem of evil"; his religious sensibility focused on that sense of sin with lasting political consequences. Only when he found inspiration in Saint Paul, who had a similar sensibility to his own, did he find a more satisfying answer than Manichaeanism provided.

A last persuasive feature of Manichaeanism was that it offered a "two-tier" doctrine of the spiritual life that could readily migrate to a Christian worldview. Manichaeanism seems on its face to demand a suicidal hostility to the material world. If the flesh is evil and the spirit good, then taking leave of the flesh by suicide seems to be the route to felicity, or at least to emancipation from earthly evil. In practice, it was held to be sufficient even for the most devout to reduce the fleshliness of existence—by sexual abstinence, eating a sparse vegetarian diet, drinking water, wearing linen garments, and avoiding the use of animal hides and fur. In the Middle Ages the Manichaean elite, the *perfecti*, followed this regime; only those who felt themselves to be particularly called to live such lives were under any obligation to do so. Most people could continue to live their usual lives: so long as we are trapped here on the material earth, we do not sin if we do not succumb unduly to greed, lust, anger, and the other sins of the flesh. Elements of this acceptance of the limits of the demands we may make on ordinary life recur throughout *The City of God*.

FROM MANICHAEANISM TO CHRISTIANITY

Augustine's account of his escape from Manichaeanism to Christianity gives Neoplatonic philosophy pride of place in making him seek nonsuperstitious intelligibility in the human predicament. It is not easy to distinguish the part played by Cicero from the part played by the Neoplatonists Plotinus and Porphyry. It is easy to believe that the deep impact of the latter was greater; they were obsessed with the same problems as Plato and reacted in the same intense, determined, and detailed way. Cicero's writings certainly had the greater impact on Augustine's ideas about politics. At nineteen he read a work of Cicero's that has long been lost and whose contents are unknown—*Hortensius*—but *The City of God* draws explicitly on Cicero's political writings: Augustine's criticism of Rome was that it suffered from the *libido dominationis*—a lust for power for its own sake that is inimical to the pursuit of even earthly justice, a complaint that comes straight from Cicero's *De republica*. In *The City of God*, the most "political" discussions come many books apart, and many years apart in their writing, when Augustine so to speak returns to the argument with Cicero that he begins in book 2 and concludes in book 21, but the argumentative method is the same: to hold Rome to Cicero's standards.

What Augustine learned from the Neoplatonists was how to reconcile the goodness of ultimate reality with the miseries of the world of everyday experience. This world is inevitably a vale of tears, for it is a shadow of the true world illuminated by the light of the divine mind. Stripped of Mani's absurd cosmogenic myths, the thought became acceptable that ultimate reality is one, perfect, indivisible, and unshakable, while the world in which we dwell is fragmentary and chaotic and incessantly shaken by disasters both natural and contrived by passionate and unwise humanity. Evil is privation, not a positive force in the world. The notion that the ultimate misfortune for humanity is separation from God is a thought of the same kind. There was room for a dialogue at least between adherents of the Christian and Jewish faith in a strongly personal God and Neoplatonists attached to the idea of a central Mind or Intelligence animating the world. Augustine himself observed that he found in his philosophical reading the insight that begins Saint John's gospel: "In the beginning was the Word, and the Word was with God, and the Word was God."[11]

Still, Augustine was converted—or reconverted— by reading Saint Paul. He had become increasingly unhappy and unsure of himself. He finally convinced himself that he had received a divine message to open the Bible and read what it commanded. He opened the book, read a passage from the Epistles, and took it as a direct injunction to arm himself with the Lord Jesus Christ. The sharpness of the break was greater at an emotional than an intellectual level, but at the emotional level it struck like a thunderbolt, which is just the impression his *Confessions* conveys. All the same, conversion implied nothing about whether Augustine should do something other than climb the career ladder to a provincial governorship. Most Christians were laymen and laywomen going about their ordinary lives; only a few became recluses or members of monastic communities. Augustine was initially inclined to become a recluse and adopt a Christian version of the quiet life led by Plotinus when he retired into the country to think. Nor did his return to Africa after the death of Monica lead immediately to the priesthood; he established a small community in Thagaste before being more or less strong-armed into the priesthood by the congregation at Hippo.

PRACTICAL POLITICS AND THEORETICAL POLITICS: THE PROVOCATION FOR *THE CITY OF GOD*

His reluctance to give up the quiet life of the scholar was genuine. Augustine would happily have kept away from the world of politics. He was combative, and his work is polemical; but the fights he picked were with those who committed intellectual, moral, and spiritual errors. He was a warrior in the cause of theological truth. This means, inter alia, that although *The City of God* is an enormous book, "a loose, baggy monster," as it has been called,[12] it is not Augustine's "political theory." That is an intellectual construction of later ages, not something Augustine created. Most of *The City of God* is concerned with theological controversies and large philosophical issues. Some of it is historical controversy. Some things that the modern world would think part of a political theory, even things one would have thought central to a Christian political theory, such as an account of the right of the state to enforce religious uniformity, hardly feature in *The City of God*. They hardly feature, because Augustine takes it for granted that it is a good thing if an earthly ruler is imbued with the true faith and is willing to bring his people to that faith. He had scruples about the means used; he did not, for instance, wish to see torture employed against the Donatists, the North African sect that threatened his church in the early 400s, even though the Donatists were themselves physically violent. But he took it for granted that earthly rulers should bring their subjects to God if they could. What else were they to do?[13]

The provocation for writing *The City of God* was the sack of Rome in 410. This did not mark "the fall of the Roman Empire"; the western empire had been militarily on the defensive for two centuries, the last emperor, the sixteen-year-old Romulus Augustus, was deposed only in 476, and elements of Roman administration persisted for another century in the west. The Byzantine Empire endured until 1453. Nor was the physical damage done to Rome by Alaric and the Visigoths particularly severe; this was not the Romans sacking Carthage. The psychological shock was another matter. Moreover, it provoked the argument about the role of Christianity in the destruction of Rome that Augustine responded to. When Christians were persecuted in earlier centuries, before the emergence of Christianity as the official religion of the empire, the reason was that their unwillingness to sacrifice to the traditional gods imperiled the state. Pagan religion ascribed earthly misfortune to the malice of gods who had been insulted or slighted, so the Christian unwillingness to sacrifice to the gods was a literal threat to the well-being of their fellow citizens.[14] It was rarely suggested that they posed any other threat—although Nero, seeking a scapegoat for the burning of Rome, latched onto the Christians as an unpopular group on whom to pin responsibility, as others did thereafter in face of a variety of disasters.

Augustine was not quick to respond to the suggestion that Christian hostility to the old gods was the deathknell for Rome. He began to write *The City of God* in 413, three years after Alaric's invaders had ransacked Rome. Whatever his immediate purposes, it turned out to be a fruitful provocation. Augustine created a Christian political theology by turning Cicero inside out. At the end of *De republica*, Cicero placed the fantasy of Scipio's Dream, a few lyrical pages that purport to record the encounter of Scipio Africanus the Younger with the first Scipio Africanus in the heavens where his spirit now dwelled. The older Scipio gave an account of the afterlife very like that which Plato provides at the end of *Republic*, and rehearsed many of the ideas on which Stoics and Neoplatonists agreed—the vanity of earthly desire, the transitoriness of human glory, and the triviality of the life of the body, among them. The passage illuminates the tension that Augustine had to handle throughout *The City of God*, though he, like Macrobius, was interested in Scipio's Dream only as a source of reflection on such topics as the transmigration of souls. In *The City of God*, it is Scipio's account of the history of Rome and his account of a true *res publica* that Augustine criticizes. Scipio the Younger was the leading speaker in *De republica*; he sets out the standards for a true *res publica* and the conditions necessary if there is to be a true *populus*, a people whose common good is served by a republic practicing earthly justice. If there is no justice, there is no *res populi*, and therefore no *res republica*. The standards of justice are universal; they are given in natural law; and natural law is known to all mankind who consult their reason. The key ideas are justice and reason; the republic is founded on justice, and the requirements of justice are known to reason. Man is distinguished from the beasts by the possession of reason, and from other gregarious creatures by being able to found a community on the practice of justice rather than sociability alone.[15]

Augustine subverts these claims by accepting them. He does not deny that man possesses reason, but by the time he began to write *The City of God*, he had ceased to believe that reason was capable of motivating human beings to behave as they ought; we have only a very limited degree of free will, and in general, he says, reason merely assists us to choose one more or less sinful course over another. Nor does Augustine deny that Cicero's account of justice is an accurate account of the nature of justice: a settled intention to give everyone his due is what justice is. What he denies is that *any* state on earth ever was, is now, or ever will be a true *res publica* in the Ciceronian sense, and therefore that any actual people can be a *populus* in the Ciceronian sense of a political community practicing real justice. *The City of God* makes two claims, one more difficult than the other. The simpler claim is that no pagan state practices Ciceronian justice, because no pagan state gives the one true God his due. By the same token, no pagan state can have a true common good, so no pagan state can be a true *res populi*. This seems an unfair and ad hoc argument, since justice between members of a political community hardly seems on all fours with justice toward God. Nonetheless, it is a useful part of a case against those who accused the Christians of bringing about the downfall of Rome by forbidding the worship of the old gods. Their complaint was that the Christian emperors who forbade the worship of the old gods had treated the old gods unjustly by depriving them of the worship that was their due; so the old gods had retaliated by withdrawing their protection from Rome. One of Augustine's best, and wholly effective, retorts was that the old gods had never kept their side of the bargain; they had never protected any state, however devotedly their adherents had kept up their cults. He lists the innumerable disasters that Rome suffered when most attached to the old cults; throughout *The City of God* he insists that good and bad fortune falls upon the just and the unjust alike.[16]

The more difficult claim is that it is not clear that even a Christian state can practice true justice, though it obviously clears the hurdle at which pagan states must, on this view, fall at once. It can give God his due by worshipping the one true God and no others. But since real justice is giving everyone what is really due to him or her, and the only being who knows what that is is God, true earthly justice is beyond us, or, at least, we cannot know whether we have achieved it. If justice is not the foundation of human affairs, what is? The reply is *love*, but love in a very difficult sense; it is tempting, though cowardly, to leave the word in Augustine's Latin, *libido*. Love, in Augustine's usage, embraces love in the ordinary sense of strong affection, and it certainly embraces sexual desire; but it also embraces the mathematician's desire to discover an elegant proof of a difficult theorem and the general's wish to win a victory. Nor is Augustine saying anything so banal as that we do what we do because we *want* to. That is true, but uninteresting. Love in Augustine's sense is an active force in the world, as we see when he claims that in any loving relationship between two people there are three agents in action: the lover, the beloved, and "love itself." *Libido*, or active desire, makes the world move, and especially the social and political world. It is important, too, that it is an active force that can take possession of us; the Rome whose misfortunes provoked the writing of *The City of God* was animated by a *libido dominandi*—a desire for conquest—that then dominated Rome herself. Just as sexual passion can become addictive, so can the desire for glory.

Augustine escaped the clutches of the Manichaean view that evil was an active force when he accepted Plotinus's view that evil is privation, a loss of good, and not a positive force. Understanding evil as estrangement from God and his grace was a Christian rendering of the Neoplatonists' claim that the world is the more evil and the more unreal the farther away it is from the One and the True. Nonetheless, Augustine did not empty the world of forces that would, if misdirected, get humanity into trouble. Love was the most important of them. Their existence did not undermine individual agency. Indeed, Augustine emphasized the individual will in ways the ancient world had not. For Augustine the problem of the will was central. He was a strong-willed person by anyone's standards; and he possessed an acute sense that he had when young deliberately willed to do wrong. This was a breach with the Platonic tradition every bit as great as identifying the impersonal "one" of Neoplatonism with the very personal God of the Old Testament. Socrates surprised his contemporaries by insisting that we do evil only in error and that it is a lack of knowledge of the good that explains human wickedness. Augustine articulated what is implicit in Saint Paul; we sin against the light because we have a will to do evil.

Some commentators have been puzzled by one of the stories that Augustine retailed in his *Confessions*.[17] When he was a boy, he and some friends stole pears from a neighbor's orchard. It was a pointless theft. The pears were no good; he had no need of them; he and his companions gave them to the pigs. The misdemeanor was doubly symbolic. It was a willful crime, committed not to get the pears but out of sheer devilment; he wanted to break the rules and committed a pointless theft to gratify that desire. Adam had no need of the apple; he said he was beguiled by Eve, but that was an evasion. He wanted to break the most important of the few rules that God had laid down for him. Why might we, or Adam, or Augustine want to behave like this? Two reasons occur to Augustine: first, simple pride. We are creatures who not only have wills but wish to make those wills effective. Why else does God afflict Job with all sorts of unmerited misfortune save to humble his pride? Not until Thomas Hobbes twelve centuries later does another thinker appear with the same eagle-eyed insight into the role of the will and the centrality of pride in our misfortunes.

The second reason is to keep company with others.

Adam was not so much "beguiled" by Eve as ready to do whatever it took to remain in her good books. We cannot survive without company. Augustine wanted the approval of the local hoodlums and joined in their wickedness. He had a surer grasp of what motivates rioters and looters in the contemporary world than commentators looking for the deep causes of unrest. He is unflinching about the fact that he chose to do what he did and that he enjoyed it. This is non-Manichaean— it was *he*, not his body, who acted—and non-Platonic— it was not a mistake but willed misbehavior. Augustine's view of the freedom of the will is difficult, and its intricacies must be evaded here; but it is worth noting that true freedom of the will, that is, the ability to choose between good and evil at will, belonged to Adam, and only between the Creation and the Fall.[18] Fallen men can only choose between evils unless they receive divine grace, and that is the unearned gift of God. Nonetheless, we make choices, and it is we who make them.

Armed with these insights, Augustine can make short work of his opponents, though he allowed himself fourteen years, twenty-two books, and twelve hundred pages of text to do it. The fall of Rome is not to be laid at the door of the Christians; Rome did not fall because the Romans' neglect of the old gods led to the gods' rejection of Rome. Much of *The City of God* focuses on that issue, though the reader is hard put to it to remember the fact, when Augustine is pursuing Roman historians through the last recesses of their narratives of the glory of Rome. He ignores innumerable traditional issues. He nowhere bothers to discuss the merits of different forms of government; Polybian or Aristotelian classification does not interest him, and he is not interested in Aristotle's great concern, the prevention of stasis. One might have expected him to be, but Augustine's world was not the Athenian polis, with its restless citizenry, but the bureaucratic empire; the empire might come to grief at the hands of invading barbarians, but it would not succumb to anything resembling stasis. In any event, trying to build an eternal polity is futile. Peace is better than war, in general and with necessary exceptions; but the preservation of perpetual peace is beyond mortal men, and they must live with that fact. Indeed, they must look only for the consolation of knowing that, in the eternal scheme of things, it is of small account whether they perish this year or in a decade's time. This deflates Roman glory, and especially Roman *libertas*: "As far as this mortal life is concerned, which is spent and finished in a few days, what difference does it make under what rule a man lives who is soon to die, provided only that those who rule him do not compel him to what is impious and wicked?"[19] Rome may have done the peoples it subjugated no real harm by conquering them, but by the same token, the glory the Romans got did them no real good.

THE CITIZENS OF THE CITY OF GOD

We must, to make complete sense of all this, start with the most obvious question. What is the city of God and who are its citizens, and what is the earthly city and who are its citizens? Augustine's answer is that the citizens of the city of God are those whom God by his grace has admitted to the company of the saved. The earthly city is defined by exclusion as the company of all the rest. The "earthly city," as much as the "city of God," is a conceptual rather than a geographical entity; Old Testament saints are citizens of the heavenly city, and so are those yet unborn who will receive God's grace in future. The population of a physical earthly city contains both the elect and the nonelect, and earthly judgment cannot be sure which is which. Election is not something we can discern with mortal eyes, or something we can earn by good behavior. We are all sinners, and God might justly have condemned all of us to eternal punishment: Augustine uses an argument that the violently reactionary critic of the French Revolution Joseph de Maistre found invaluable fourteen centuries later. Voltaire had asked why God chose to destroy Lisbon in the earthquake of 1755; was there not dancing and misbehavior in Paris too? Maistre's reply is Augustine's. None of us is innocent of the sin of Adam. A godless pride is built into us at birth. We talk of childish innocence, but babies are not innocent. They are weak; the red-faced baby longing for its mother's breast and bawling fit to burst its lungs is powerless to wreak upon the world the violence it would like to wreak in its frustration.[20] The content of its desires is as bad as could be. When God saves some but allows many to suffer eternal punishment, it is not his sin but theirs that explains why they are punished. We should be grateful that he has spared some when he might in justice have punished all.

We mortal spectators here below cannot know who is a member of the city of God; not the least powerful of the implications is that political relationships cannot be based on distinguishing the saved and the elect. Augustine's insistence on the mixed nature of all human communities was a powerful argument in the local conflicts of his own day, but equally important in explaining the nature of Christian politics. In insisting that any ruler who provided the limited earthly goods that a state could provide was entitled to our obedience, Augustine provided the foundations of two famous arguments, both controversial. The first was the view of Aquinas that Christians must obey non-Christian rulers; the second was what became in seventeenth-century Europe the highly unpopular claim that a Christian commonwealth should be governed in the same way as any other commonwealth.[21] The local problems that provoked him were specific to his time and region. The great threat to the unity of the Catholic Church in Africa was posed by the so-called Donatists, named after a bishop of Carthage—Donatus the Great—who was their leader in the mid-fourth century. They were extreme rigorists, who wanted a church of the elect alone. Their standard of election was a person's conduct during the last of the persecutions. They denied that anyone who had succumbed to persecution was entitled to give the sacraments; and they insisted on rebaptizing members of their sect.

The Donatists were condemned many times by imperial edicts and church councils, became more extreme in the face of persecution, and by the end of the fourth century convinced themselves they were the only Christian church in all the world, and entitled to convert dissenters by force. They occupied twenty years of Augustine's time as bishop and were a sore trial to his spirit. They also made him more ready to employ the brute force of the state to bring heretics to obedience than when he first took office. They were not the only unamenable sect to plague Augustine; the Circumcellions—the name means simply "those who live in the neighboring villages"—

were a still more violent offshoot of the Donatists. Their political interest is that they forced him to articulate clearly the view that it is the sacrament, not the minister, that is efficacious: what matters is the sacrament being administered and not the moral purity of the minister. This is not a directly political view, but it has clear political implications: if what matters is the law and its effects, we should not inquire into the character of political leaders but look to their impact on the lives of their subjects.

Augustine's doctrine of the mixed quality of all human communities—the Catholic Church included—meant that no earthly body could claim to be "the city of God on earth" and that although Christian asceticism was acceptable—he himself lived with a community of celibates from the moment he became a priest—it did nothing to lessen the contrast between the mixed earthly community and the city of the saved. A community of ascetics could not lay claim to be a community of the elect. This had large implications for the authority of the church vis-à-vis the state. Augustine had no doubt that it was the task of the church to warn rulers as well as their subjects when they were acting immorally; not to do so was to commit an injustice toward them, since admonition was their due.[22] In general, however, the church ought not to exercise earthly responsibilities. This did not mean that the functionaries of the church might not also have to perform secular administrative duties. Augustine knew that de facto the empire could not function unless bishops took responsibility for hearing civil cases in their dioceses, and since emperors had placed this burden upon them, they were obliged to discharge these duties to the extent consistent with the Christian faith. It meant that the church as an institution should attend primarily to its one unique function, caring for the souls of its members, although caring for the unfortunate and the destitute was a Christian duty, too.

Augustine had to steer a careful path. Christ told his followers to render unto Caesar the things that were Caesar's. They were to pay taxes and obey the civil authorities in everything not contrary to the direct injunctions of Christ; by the time of Augustine, the pacifism of the early church had been transcended, and it was agreed that if Christians were recruited to fight in the imperial armies, they must do so. Nonetheless, they were not to embroil themselves in politics. They were not to resist tyrants, nor were they to disobey their lawful rulers except under very extreme circumstances, and then only by passive disobedience. Only when they were given a command that in effect amounted to the requirement to deny Christ, might they refuse. Martyrdom occurred in all persecutions when those suspected of Christian attachments were required to sacrifice to the pagan Gods and eat the sacrificial meat, or required to swear allegiance to the cult of the emperor. Swearing allegiance to the emperor's cult was regarded by the civic authorities as the *least* demanding declaration of civic loyalty they could ask of a Roman subject, but it was a sticking point for both Jews and Christians. Augustine thought that if they were so required, they had to, if they had the strength, refuse and endure the consequences. On no account were they to engage in rebellion, incite tyrannicide, or disturb the earthly peace of the empire.[23]

One need only recall the way in which Cicero's writings are replete with praise for tyrannicides, including the murderers of the Gracchi, himself in the case of Catiline's followers, and subsequently the murderers of Julius Caesar, to see the gulf that has opened up between the classical and the Christian political universe. The reasons need no rehearsing, but vast as these differences are, we must not exaggerate their implications. Cicero's thinking is this-worldly, Augustine's other-worldly; Cicero's republic is worthy of respect, admiration, and loyalty, and its glory is a great good, but Augustine thinks all earthly states are the playgrounds of violent and self-deluded men, and earthly glory mere vanity. The temptation that we must resist is to conclude that Augustine has nothing good to say about earthly life and that the state is to be regarded with contempt.

POLITICS AS A LIMITED GOOD

This is wrong. The world is God's creation. To despise it is blasphemous. Augustine did not follow classical philosophers in their wholesale contempt for the body. They elevated mind and, in so doing, deprecated body. Given his extraordinary intelligence, he had no need to do the first, and he was not tempted to do the second. He was certainly curious about the body. One of the things that has given rise to the belief that he was obsessed with sex is his recurrent discussion of the contrast between pre-Fall Adam, who would have had sexual intercourse with Eve for the sake of friendship and mutual affection, and would have had an erect penis when and only when he wanted one, and fallen man, who is driven by lust, has erections when he does not want them, and cannot have them when he wants them.[24] He was not in fact concerned with sexual continence to anything like the extent to which he was concerned with deceit, malice, and plain brutality.

What the curious case of the male sexual organs demonstrates is the way in which we—that is, the fallen male we—cannot control what we very much want to control. The disunity of mind and body is a fact of deep significance. Nor did he confine these thoughts to the case of men. He made a point of arguing that the women who were raped by Alaric's Visigoths in the sack of Rome were not violated and not dishonored; there was all the difference in the world between being the victim of rape and the instigator of fornication. Even if some of them had found themselves sexually excited against their will, they were not to feel ashamed—this is one of the cases where the body acts of its own accord. As to the Roman heroine Lucretia, who committed suicide after being raped by Tarquin, Augustine claimed that she was doubly wrong—wrong to think herself dishonored by the rape and wrong to kill herself. Raped, she was an innocent victim of assault; in committing suicide, she had killed an innocent woman and was a real murderess. Augustine discussed Lucretia at what even he agreed was perhaps excessive length, but uses this, and many other examples where Roman historians and poets had praised a suicide, to argue that suicide was murder—not to be admired but deplored.[25]

The earthly kingdom exists to promote peace in this world. The goods of this world are as nothing to the ultimate good of union with God, but they are not to be despised. Peace on earth is as nothing to the peace we shall enjoy in the company of God, but peace is a very great good. We and the world we live in are God's creations. While we live here below, we must accommodate ourselves to its reality. One such reality is the impotence of religion to fend off earthly evil. The

Christians were not responsible for the downfall of Rome, and Mars was not responsible for Rome's glory. Earthly success and failure have earthly causes. God's misfortunes rightly fall upon the just and the unjust alike, and to seek the proximate cause of disaster in local wickedness is an error. The larger claim, one to which Augustine recurs throughout *The City of God*, is that even the success of Rome was not something to glory in. States exist because we care for earthly things and require earthly arrangements to satisfy that desire. Property, to take the central worldly institution that the state protects, has a limited but real value. Without laws governing *meum et tuum*, there would be dissension and bloodshed, and starvation into the bargain. All the same, property has a relative value only, and its side effects are unattractive, including as they do greed and cupidity and opportunities for theft.[26] Without a state there could be no stable ownership, so the existence of political and legal arrangements of the minimal kind required to sustain the rule of law, and an economy adequate to keep us fed and sheltered, is desirable.

Such a regime cannot achieve *ultimate* justice; that is, it does not give to everyone what is really due to him or her, not least because that will not be known until the last judgment; but as institutions built on our love of earthly things and taking advantage of nothing more than our intelligence to coordinate our behavior in the interests of our long-run welfare rather than our short-run impulses, property and the legal institutions that maintain it are to be valued. If we may not kill ourselves, we ought not to neglect ourselves, either; so ordinary legal or conventional justice is to be valued and conscientiously pursued. Augustine makes life difficult for the reader because he moves back and forth between agreeing that "there was, of course, according to a more practicable definition, a commonwealth of a sort; and it was certainly better administered by the Romans of more ancient times than by those who have come after them,"[27] and reiterating his negative reply to the question "Whether there ever was a Roman commonwealth answering to the definitions proposed by Scipio in Cicero's dialogue."[28] The negative reply rests as always on the thought that no society can give a man his due if it takes him away from the worship of the one true God. A godless republic is no *res publica*. Since the only *res populi* that matters is the worship of the one true God, a polity devoted to the worship of demons has no *res populi*, and the multitude of whom it is composed is no true *populus*. Viewed in that light, the only true *populus* are the citizens of the city of God. Viewed more "practicably," earthly justice is self-evidently better than injustice.

Rome did not confine itself to the rational pursuit of earthly but not overrated interests; Rome conquered the world. Contrary to Polybius and Cicero, who thought the Roman Republic of the midsecond century BCE was the height of political success, Augustine almost invariably attacks the whole enterprise as driven by the *libido dominandi*, the lust for conquest. Like Plato, he thought imperial ambition was a self-destructive folly. If human beings had been rational, they would have created not empires but an enormous number of very small states—Augustine says *regna*, literally "kingdoms," but he means any set of political arrangements whatever. A multitude of tiny, harmless polities could have lived at peace among themselves and therefore at peace internally, just as a city contains innumerable households, none of which seeks to dominate the others, and all of which may be domestically at peace.[29] This was not the revival of Christian pacifism. Augustine freely admits that there are just wars and thinks it a grave sin not to fight them when we should. Nonetheless, it is a rather astonishing suggestion, even if one might think the example of the Greek city-states of antiquity suggests that large numbers of small states is not a reliable recipe for peaceful coexistence.

THE STATE, PUNISHMENT, AND JUST WAR

The central feature of the state is that it wields coercive power. Private individuals can cajole and entreat; the

state can issue orders and back up those orders by violence against the recalcitrant. Punishment serves two
purposes. The threat of punishment gives bad people a
motive to behave better. Their wills may only be amenable to earthly inducements, but against the attractions of misconduct we can set the dissuasion of earthly
penalties and thereby promote peace. Since the Fall we
have only limited free will, but Augustine does not
underestimate the possibility that with appropriate aids
we can avoid choosing the more obvious and antisocial
evils. The ultimate cause of the existence of political
societies is sin; absent the Fall, we might live in simple,
egalitarian, communist communities with neither property, nor law, nor political authority. Our fallen nature
needs regulation. Augustine's day-to-day conduct in his
little celibate community certainly suggests that he
thought that both reproof and encouragement could
strengthen the wills of his fellows in the direction of
good and away from evil, and that is what he argues in
The City of God.[30] If threats fail, punishment may reform
the criminal. Because Augustine hoped for the reformation of the criminal, he was hostile to the death penalty.
He was unflinching about the brutality of the Roman
state, but his understanding of the purpose of punishment made the death penalty simply wrong. The inflic-
tion of punishment is an educative process. Like the
father chastising his son to get him into the good habits

that will regulate his conduct without the need for further chastisement, the state that imposes successful punishment will train the criminal into better behavior. If the better behavior becomes habitual, there will be no need for further punishment. To kill a man deprives him of the possibility of repentance.[31]

Augustine's argument goes deeper than this, with regard both to the criminal and to the court and the executioner. The criminal is supposed to be brought to a state of repentance, but Augustine thinks it almost impossible for him to die in a good frame of mind. Given the barbarity of Roman executions, that seems all too plausible. The argument is backed by other considerations. In Roman criminal procedure, accused persons were commonly "put to the question," which is to say tortured until they gave what were perceived by their interrogators as honest answers; and material witnesses could expect the same treatment. The privilege that a Roman citizen most valued was that a citizen was not tortured for his evidence. Augustine was passionate that nobody should be condemned unjustly. He thought the judge's task was hideous at the best of times. Since certainty was not to be had, the judge could never be sure that he had done (earthly) justice. Sentencing a man to flogging or execution for a crime he had not committed was something that Augustine shuddered at. The same reasoning applied to the criminal. An innocent man might endure torture without incriminating himself, only to die of the torture; or he might incriminate himself falsely to spare himself the pain of further torture. To kill an innocent man or to force an innocent man to perjure himself was an appalling evil. These evils lay squarely on the conscience of the judge, and Augustine is more appalled by the impact of sin on our souls than by the torments inflicted upon the body.

This is not the expression of a modern humanitarian impulse. The extent of modern humanitarianism is in any case debatable; we have more in common with Romans who enjoyed seeing criminals torn to pieces by wild beasts than we like to acknowledge. Augustine did not flinch from physical suffering; and hypocrisy was wholly foreign to him. He did not flinch from the *fact* of the hangman or the soldier or the civilian police. It no doubt took a peculiar temperament to earn a living by butchering one's fellow human beings, but it did not follow that the hangman was not God's instrument. In this vale of sorrows, he is. Nor should we, looking back from a safe distance, ignore the fact that corporal and capital punishments are almost inescapable in societies where the expense of housing and feeding prisoners would be intolerable, and where only the better-off would have had the resources to pay fines—as they frequently did. The violent poor would suffer violence at the hands of the state, as would poor robbers and housebreakers. Augustine's fear was not that they would suffer but that they would suffer for what they had not done.

Given such a view of punishment, it was possible to imagine the state acting like a stern father, compelling a reluctant offspring to toe the line. This view of punishment provides the premises for Augustine's account of just war, which has been immensely influential, even though it partly rests on an analogy between the state's right to punish its own members and its right to punish other states, an analogy that the modern world largely rejects. The most familiar parts of the case are very familiar indeed. Self-defense is always a legitimate ground for fighting, and nobody should hesitate to fight back when attacked; self-defense is always a valid casus belli. Nor need we wait until the enemy is literally at the gates before we resist; we may frustrate his preparations for attack as well. These claims became part of the standard account of just war doctrine in the later Middle Ages and are enshrined in modern doctrine, to the extent of featuring in the Charter of the United Nations. The less usual claim is that in a just war a state punishes the crimes of another state and its people. On the face of it, this seems to involve a notion of collective guilt otherwise foreign to Augustine and a willingness to see the innocent die that seems at odds with his condemnation of the death penalty. The state acts, so to speak, in the name of global justice—due precaution taken about the extent to which we can achieve here below anything properly called justice, and how far Augustine thought that there was a law of peoples that conferred such a right—or duty.

A just war is motivated by the intention to give to each what is his due, in this case the punishment due to an aggressor. The idea that a state should act to promote justice was not at odds with Roman ideas; it was at odds with what Augustine thought had in fact motivated Rome. There was an old Roman tradition of not going to war in the absence of a casus belli, a quasi-legal justification for an attack, which was in reality an equally old tradition of manufacturing situations to produce the necessary excuse. There is an obvious rhetorical awkwardness in Augustine's insisting on the inadequacy of earthly justice while defending what we cannot but call a "just war," much as there is an awkwardness when he emphasizes that there is no *real* justice here below at the same time that he insists that we must play our part in the institutions that administer "justice," such as the courts, police, and prisons. But Augustine is, after all, talking of both the city of God, the community of the saved that is here on earth only as a "pilgrim," as well as the earthly city, and he quite rightly reminds us that this world is not just as the heavenly city will be just and that our capacity to determine the deserts of states and individuals is limited.[32]

There is a further twist to Augustine's position. Unlike his predecessors such as Cicero and almost equally bleak successors such as Thomas Hobbes, Augustine believed that we are sinners. Cicero thought many Romans behaved badly, but he did not discuss this in terms of "sin." Hobbes thought we were provoked into harming one another in the absence of secure government and often behaved badly for reasons such as pride; but he expressly repudiated the idea of original sin. For Augustine original sin is the most important fact about us. Some are saved and some are not, but all are sinners. This puts a distinctive complexion on what would in the absence of the framework provided by the doctrine of original sin be a grim, pessimistic, this-worldly, and empirically wholly plausible outlook on political authority and political life. In the absence of government, with its attendant apparatus of law and law enforcement, we cannot help behaving badly because we are terrified of being robbed, assaulted, or murdered by other people; where there is no government and no law enforcement, we are rationally tempted to make a preemptive strike and attack them before they can attack us—the knowledge of which increases their fear of us and makes it more likely that they will attack us preemptively. That is Hobbes.

Absent original sin, this vicious circle is broken by the institution of government. We shall not be afraid of others if we know that they are afraid of the law; and they will not fear us when they know that we, too, are afraid of the law. We are a threat to one another because we fear one another; when that fear is removed, we can become peaceful and cooperative creatures. Augustine anticipates every step of this (Hobbesian) argument, but he cannot stop there. One could say that he pauses there when he admits that, "in a practicable sense," Rome at its best practiced (a sort of) earthly justice; but if he pauses, he does not stop there. If humanity was as coolly and self-controlledly rational as this argument suggests, our history would be infinitely less unhappy than it has been. Our problem is that we suffer from what one might call surplus motivation toward theft and violence—namely, the wickedness that stems from original sin. The boy who stole pears out of devilment is a younger version of the men who rob their neighbors and invade other countries for loot and for glory. This is the sin that Augustine identifies as the sin that drove Adam to take the apple; the apple was neither here nor there. The self-will that led to its taking was. Augustine praises the state for quelling violence and robbery, but reminds us that the drive toward violence and robbery is still there—not cured, only counteracted.

For Augustine, then, the sense that the earthly city

is the city of those driven by love of earthly things is pervasive; he had few reasons to explain at length which earthly cities are better than which others, and why, though it was clear that some were much better than others. It is obvious that peace and good order are good; obvious that chaos and war are bad. That almost exhausts the comparison. Relatively good earthly cities are not in the deepest sense just, but "well ordered." This is a powerful thought, and an elegant kidnapping of an idea usually more at home in the thinking of republicans. The "well-ordered" republic that Machiavelli and Rousseau longed for was an idealized version of the republic described by Cicero, and hankered after by the founders of the American Republic. In Augustine's discussion, mixed republics and well-founded states are at no particular advantage. Augustine thinks *any* state can be "well-ordered" so long as there is peace, agreements are kept, laws are observed, and affairs are predictable. Rousseau's claim that when an absolute monarchy achieves these things, we achieve the silence of the graveyard would have struck Augustine as romantic nonsense.

To the modern eye, one further disconcerting and interesting element in Augustine's accounts of just war, of punishment, and of the individual's relationship to the state is the insistence that the individual must leave politics to the powers that be. Augustine's grounds for insisting that we must not resist our rulers under (almost) any circumstances are interesting and, it must be said, dangerous. They are at odds with almost everything other writers have said on the subject. Hobbes insisted that we must obey our sovereign in anything that did not threaten our lives; in what did threaten our lives, we must do what we could to save ourselves. This is not a doctrine of *resistance*, as in Locke, let alone tyrannicide, as in Cicero. Locke allows us to resist the sovereign when he violates the compact that establishes his authority; Cicero think tyrants are criminals and should be killed. Hobbes held the wholly secular view that no state can survive if individuals are free to pick and choose which rules to obey, so we must obey our rulers unless our life is imperiled. Augustine anticipates the secular argument, but his conviction that it does not matter very much whether we die sooner or later means that he does not rely on the right of self-defense to uphold a "last-ditch" right to disobey our rulers. Augustine accepted the Pauline claim that the powers that be are ordained by God and that disobedience—save under the conditions spelled out earlier—is an affront to God.

Nonetheless, this is not a defense of the divine right of kings, and not a defense of theocracy—not an argument for giving priests political power. Augustine does not argue, as later writers did, that kings are the Lord's anointed and that their right to govern is *personal*; his argument is only that God has created rulers whose power is part of the providential order, and must be accepted as such. The bleakness of the argument is extreme. One can see how bleak it is by considering the famous tag in book 4 of *The City of God*: "if justice is absent, what is a state other than a large and successful band of robbers?" Augustine says that even robbers must observe some of the rules of justice in order to prosecute their schemes successfully; and robbers know as well as anyone else that robbery is wrong and unjust, since they themselves do not wish to be robbed. All this has led many commentators to draw the obvious inference that Augustine is following Cicero in arguing that what defines a true state is that it is based on justice. Since orderly coordination even for wicked purposes requires justice, how much more so an organization created for good purposes?

If Augustine had gone down that track, he would have been more plausible but less original and interesting than he was. Some states would have been nothing more than *magna latrocinia*—large and successful bands of robbers—and others would have been lawful regimes founded on justice. The Nazi regime would have been the former and Britain and the United States the latter. Augustine did not do the obvious thing. He quoted with pleasure the brave—or foolhardy—response of a captured pirate to Alexander the Great. Asked by the great conqueror what he meant by his piracy, he replied that he meant just the same as Alexander, and that he took it amiss that just because Alexander had many ships and he had only one, he was condemned as a pirate and Alexander was praised as a hero. Augustine's view seems rather to be that states are by nature *magna latrocinia*, but that under their protection the limited goods of this earthly life can be pursued.

In short, the authentic Augustinian note is that states are organizations built to allow the earthly passions of human beings to be satisfied without excessive disorder. These passions always tend toward disorder, and no amount of law will put an end to that. Punishment and the threat of punishment can bend men's wills in the right direction, even though it is only because we care so much for life, liberty, and property that we are amenable to threats of death, imprisonment, and fines. Generally speaking, states are indeed much the same as large bands of robbers; substantial states get into wars and are animated by the lust for domination. More sensible and less passionate creatures than we would have lived in innumerable small, self-centered, and self-satisfied states and would not have got into the fights we have. But just as cowardly bishops can administer the sacraments, and we are not to inquire into their characters but accept the sacraments at their hands, earthly rulers must be obeyed because they are rulers and not because they are good men. If we have benign and merciful rulers, we are lucky; if not, we cannot complain. The deficiency of this view is that it offers no defense against genocidal madmen such as Hitler and Stalin other than the reflection that they will in due course come to grief: little consolation to their victims.

If he does not encourage resistance when one wishes that he had, Augustine equally takes no advantage of the potential for toleration and religious liberty inherent in his own ideas. Consider the way in which his distaste for the death penalty owed so much to his wish that in struggles between the Catholic Church and its rivals—especially the Donatists in Africa—the losing party should come around to the opinion of the victors and should be brought back into the fold by love and by argument. At a personal level, he seems eventually to have become exasperated with the Donatists. Who would not have lost patience with people who resorted to violence and intimidation to make converts and reduce the ranks of the Catholics, and who denied the right of the secular authorities to regulate their affairs while constantly appealing to the imperial authorities for judgment in their favor and refusing to take condemnation for an answer? The Circumcellions were worse. It is not surprising that he urged the secular authorities to suppress them.

The personal element in Augustine's reactions is not important. More important is this: Augustine's account of the limited utility of the earthly city, taken in conjunction with everything he says about the mixed nature of all earthly associations, including the church, leads naturally and readily to the thought that the task of the state is to care for externals—to keep the peace, to regulate property, and to perform useful tasks such as providing lawcourts to settle disputes. Deep matters, questions of the meaning of life and the ultimate rewards of virtue, must be settled elsewhere. Coercion is the natural and proper instrument of the state, but force is not an argument. We can frighten people into behaving as we wish, but we cannot frighten them into an unforced belief in what we wish. Eventually, this was the soil that nourished the Protestant conception of toleration; the church is a voluntary organization for worship in common and the discussion of matters of faith, while the state is a coercive and nonvoluntary organization for the regulation of external matters.

Augustine would have found these conclusions almost unintelligible. He was heir to the pagans who feared that Christian hostility to the cults of the gods would bring disaster upon the Roman state. He drew the line at employing extreme measures of coercion, and especially at employing the death penalty because of its terminal quality. Nonetheless, although one might regard him as the very remote founder of Protestantism, he never contemplated the suggestion that religion was in any way "off-limits" to state control. This was hardly surprising. The modern idea of toleration was more than a thousand years away, and it made headway as much because of European exhaustion after the religious wars of the sixteenth and seventeenth centuries as because of the acceptance of a new principle. Roman emperors automatically protected religious institutions, and the church had now become the beneficiary rather than the victim of the policy.

The dangerous novelty was the extension of coercion from enforcing outward observance to the suppression of heresy; neither Socrates nor the victims of God's wrath in the Old Testament had been accused of heresy. One could be put to death for blasphemy, for outraging the gods, and for worshipping the wrong gods; but the concept of heresy was a distinctively Christian invention. The danger it posed was that it allowed Christians to persecute one another with a clear conscience. Augustine took it for granted that being coerced into receiving the truth was a benefit, not a burden; it was a view one might expect from a man who thought that corporal punishment might be administered lovingly and with the intention to bring the offender to his senses. Whether it was consistent with the sharp line he drew between body and soul when arguing that the women who had been raped by Alaric's soldiers remained unviolated, because accidents to the body did not impugn the integrity of the soul, is another matter. Whether, indeed, it was a plausible view, coming from the pen of the man who remembered that he had been more willing to receive a savage beating than to learn Greek, is also another matter. It became part of Christian orthodoxy. The acceptability of coerced orthodoxy to Christians relied almost entirely on Christ's injunction to "compel them to come in," and the Augustine who strained to read Christ's injunction to "turn the other cheek" in a metaphorical and spiritual sense, in order to permit Christians to serve in the military with a good conscience, now strained to read the *cogere intrare* of the parable of the reluctant wedding guests in the most literal sense to explain why earthly rulers might—indeed must—compel orthodoxy among their subjects. It was a dangerous legacy: not only did it place the Christian subject at the mercy of his ruler's ideas about what was and was not heresy; it made it inevitable that the church would claim to police the Christian ruler's orthodoxy, and inevitable that rulers would resist.

NOTES

1. Romans 13:1–7.

2. Augustine, *The City of God against the Pagans*, trans. R. W. Dyson (Cambridge: Cambridge University Press, 2001) (21.14), p. 1072.

3. Peter Brown, *Augustine of Hippo* (London: Faber & Faber, 1966), p. 39.

4. Ibid., pp. 151ff.

5. Judith Herrin, *The Formation of Christendom* (Princeton: Princeton University Press, 1987).

6. John Dewey, *A Common Faith*, vol. 9 of *Later Works* (Carbondale: Southern Illinois University Press, 1986), pp. 3–20.

7. Robin Lane Fox, *Pagans and Christians* (New York: Knopf, 1987), emphasizes the point throughout.

8. Brown, *Augustine of Hippo*, pp. 35ff.

9. Augustine, *Confessions*, trans. Henry Chadwick (Oxford: Oxford University Press, 1991) (5.5–10), pp. 76–85.

10. Ibid. (1.10), p. 9.

11. Ibid. (7.9–13), pp. 121–26.

12. By Peter Brown, quoted in the introduction to *City of God*, p. xiv.

13. Augustine, *City of God* (5.24), pp. 231–32.

14. Lane Fox, *Pagans and Christians*, pp. 37ff.

15. Cicero, *On the Commonwealth and On the Laws*, ed. James E. G. Zetzel (Cambridge: Cambridge University

Press, 1999), pp. 59–60.

16. Augustine, *City of God* (1.9), pp. 13ff.

17. Augustine, *Confessions* (2.9–17), pp. 28–34.

18. Augustine, *City of God* (14.26), pp. 628–29.

19. Ibid. (5.17), p. 217.

20. Augustine, *Confessions* (1.7), p. 9.

21. Thomas Hobbes, *Leviathan*, ed. Richard Tuck (Cambridge: Cambridge University Press, 1991), chaps. 30 et seq.

22. Augustine, *City of God* (5.26), p. 235.

23. Ibid.

24. Ibid (14.23–24), pp. 623–27.

25. Ibid. (1.19–20), pp. 29–33.

26. Ibid.

27. Ibid. (2.21), p. 80.

28. Ibid. (19.21), pp. 950–52.

29. Ibid (4.15), p. 161.

30. Ibid. (19.6), p. 928.

31. Ibid (19.16), pp. 944–45.

32. Ibid. (19.6), pp. 926–28.

Selections

THE CITY OF GOD

As the introduction stressed at some length, The City of God *is not a work of political theory, for all its impact on political thinking. I have interpolated a few sentences below to place the extracts selected here in their context in the book. Sometimes, the context is too obvious to bear further explanation.*

PREFACE

EXPLAINING HIS DESIGN IN UNDERTAKING THIS WORK

The glorious city of God is my theme in this work, which you, my dearest son Marcellinus, suggested, and which is due to you by my promise. I have undertaken its defence against those who prefer their own gods to the Founder of this city—a city surpassingly glorious, whether we view it as it still lives by faith in this fleeting

course of time, and sojourns as a stranger in the
midst of the ungodly, or as it shall dwell in the fixed
stability of its eternal seat, which it now with patience
waits for, expecting until "righteousness shall return
unto judgment," and it obtain, by virtue of its excel-
lence, final victory and perfect peace. A great work
this, and an arduous; but God is my helper. For I am
aware what ability is requisite to persuade the proud
how great is the virtue of humility, which raises us,
not by a quite human arrogance, but by a divine
grace, above all earthly dignities that totter on this
shifting scene. For the King and Founder of this city
of which we speak, has in Scripture uttered to His
people a dictum of the divine law in these words:
"God resisteth the proud, but giveth grace unto the
humble." But this, which is God's prerogative, the
inflated ambition of a proud spirit also affects, and
dearly loves that this be numbered among its attri-
butes, to

- "Show pity to the humbled soul,
- And crush the sons of pride."

And therefore, as the plan of this work we have undertaken requires, and as occasion offers, we must speak
also of the earthly city, which, though it be mistress of
the nations, is itself ruled by its lust of rule.

Augustine is aware that if the pagan gods did not protect their worshippers, the Christian God did not go out of his way to save Christians.

BOOK I

CHAPTER II

OF THE END OF THIS LIFE, WHETHER IT IS

MATERIAL THAT IT BE LONG DELAYED

But, it is added, many Christians were slaughtered, and were put to death in a hideous variety of cruel ways. Well, if this be hard to bear, it is assuredly the common lot of all who are born into this life. Of this at least I am certain, that no one has ever died who was not destined to die some time. Now the end of life puts the longest life on a par with the shortest. For of two things which have alike ceased to be, the one is not better, the other worse—the one greater, the other less. And of what consequence is it what kind of death puts an end to life, since he who has died once is not forced to go through the same ordeal a second time? And as in the daily casualties of life every man is, as it were, threatened with numberless deaths, so long as it remains uncertain which of them is his fate, I would ask whether it is not better to suffer one and die, than to live in fear of all? I am not unaware of the poor-spirited fear which prompts us to choose rather to live long in fear of so many deaths, than to die once and so escape them all; but the weak and cowardly shrinking of the flesh is one thing, and the well-considered and reasonable persuasion of the soul quite another. That death is not to be judged an evil which is the end of a good life; for death becomes evil only by the retribution which follows it. They, then, who are destined to die, need not be careful to inquire what death they are to die, but into what place death will usher them. And since Christians are well aware that the death of the godly pauper whose sores the dogs licked was far better than of the wicked rich man who lay in purple and fine linen, what harm could these terrific deaths do to the dead who had lived well?

Augustine dwells at some length on the Roman veneration of Lucretia, who killed herself after being raped by Tarquin. He argues that she was innocent until she killed herself, an act that amounted to murder.

CHAPTER 17

OF SUICIDE COMMITTED THROUGH
FEAR OF PUNISHMENT OR DISHONOR

And consequently, even if some of these virgins killed themselves to avoid such disgrace, who that has any human feeling would refuse to forgive them? And as for those who would not put an end to their lives, lest they might seem to escape the crime of another by a sin of their own, he who lays this to their charge as a great wickedness is himself not guiltless of the fault of folly. For if it is not lawful to take the law into our own hands, and slay even a guilty person, whose death no public sentence has warranted, then certainly he who kills himself is a homicide, and so much the guiltier of his own death, as he was more innocent of that offence for which he doomed himself to die. Do we justly execrate the deed of Judas, and does truth itself pronounce that by hanging himself he rather aggravated than expiated the guilt of that most iniquitous betrayal, since, by despairing of God's mercy in his sorrow that wrought death, he left to himself no place for a healing penitence? How much more ought he to abstain from laying violent hands on himself who has done nothing worthy of such a punishment! For Judas, when he killed himself, killed a wicked man; but he passed from this life chargeable not only with the death of Christ, but with his own: for though he killed himself on account of his crime, his killing himself was another crime. Why, then, should a man who has done no ill do ill to himself, and by killing himself kill the innocent to escape another's guilty act, and perpetrate upon himself a sin

of his own, that the sin of another may not be perpetrated on him?

CHAPTER 18

OF THE VIOLENCE WHICH MAY BE DONE TO
THE BODY BY ANOTHER'S LUST, WHILE
THE MIND REMAINS INVIOLATE

But is there a fear that even another's lust may pollute
the violated? It will not pollute, if it be another's: if it
pollute, it is not another's, but is shared also by the pol-
luted. But since purity is a virtue of the soul, and has for
its companion virtue, the fortitude which will rather
endure all ills than consent to evil; and since no one,
however magnanimous and pure, has always the disposal of his own body, but can control only the consent
and refusal of his will, what sane man can suppose that,
if his body be seized and forcibly made use of to satisfy
the lust of another, he thereby loses his purity? For if
purity can be thus destroyed, then assuredly purity is
no virtue of the soul; nor can it be numbered among
those good things by which the life is made good, but
among the good things of the body, in the same cate-
gory as strength, beauty, sound and unbroken health,
and, in short, all such good things as may be diminished without at all diminishing the goodness and rec-
titude of our life. But if purity be nothing better than
these, why should the body be perilled that it may be

preserved? If, on the other hand, it belongs to the soul, then not even when the body is violated is it lost. Nay more, the virtue of holy continence, when it resists the uncleanness of carnal lust, sanctifies even the body, and therefore when this continence remains unsubdued, even the sanctity of the body is preserved, because the will to use it holily remains, and, so far as lies in the body itself, the power also.

For the sanctity of the body does not consist in the integrity of its members, nor in their exemption from all touch; for they are exposed to various accidents which do violence to and wound them, and the surgeons who administer relief often perform operations that sicken the spectator. A midwife, suppose, has (whether maliciously or accidentally, or through unskillfulness) destroyed the virginity of some girl, while endeavoring to ascertain it: I suppose no one is so foolish as to believe that, by this destruction of the integrity of one organ, the virgin has lost anything even of her bodily sanctity. And thus, so long as the soul keeps this firmness of purpose which sanctifies even the body, the violence done by another's lust makes no impression on this bodily sanctity, which is preserved intact by one's own persistent continence. Suppose a virgin violates the oath she has sworn to God, and goes to meet her seducer with the intention of yielding to him, shall we say that as she goes she is possessed even of bodily sanctity, when already she has lost and destroyed that sanctity of soul which sanctifies the body? Far be it from us to so misapply words. Let us rather draw this conclusion, that while the sanctity of the soul remains even when the body is violated, the sanctity of the body is not lost; and that, in like manner, the sanctity of the body is lost when the sanctity of the soul is violated, though the body itself remains intact. And therefore a woman who has been violated by the sin of another, and without any consent of her own, has no cause to put herself to death; much less has she cause to commit suicide in order to avoid such violation, for in that case she commits certain homicide to prevent a crime which is uncertain as yet, and not her own.

CHAPTER 19

OF LUCRETIA, WHO PUT AN END TO HER LIFE
BECAUSE OF THE OUTRAGE DONE HER

This, then, is our position, and it seems sufficiently lucid. We maintain that when a woman is violated while her soul admits no consent to the iniquity, but remains inviolably chaste, the sin is not hers, but his who violates her. But do they against whom we have to defend not only the souls, but the sacred bodies too of these outraged Christian captives—do they, perhaps, dare to dispute our position? But all know how loudly they extol the purity of Lucretia, that noble matron of ancient Rome. When King Tarquin's son had violated her body, she made known the wickedness of this young profligate to her husband Collatinus, and to Brutus her kinsman, men of high rank and full of courage, and bound them by an oath to avenge it. Then, heart-sick, and unable to bear the shame, she put an end to her life. What shall we call her? An adulteress, or chaste? There is no question which she was. Not more happily than truly did a declaimer say of this sad occurrence: "Here was a marvel: there were two, and only one committed adultery." Most forcibly and truly spoken. For this declaimer, seeing in the union of the two bodies the foul lust of the one, and the chaste will of the other, and giving heed not to the contact of the bodily members, but to the wide diversity of their souls, says: "There were two, but the adultery was committed only by one."

But how is it, that she who was no partner to the crime bears the heavier punishment of the two? For the adulterer was only banished along with his father; she suffered the extreme penalty. If that was not impurity by which she was unwillingly ravished, then this is not justice by which she, being chaste, is punished. To you I appeal, ye laws and judges of Rome. Even after the perpetration of great enormities, you do not suffer the criminal to be slain untried. If, then, one were to bring to your bar this case, and were to prove to you that a woman not only untried, but chaste and innocent, had been killed, would you not visit the murderer with punishment proportionably severe? This crime was committed by Lucretia; that Lucretia so celebrated and lauded slew the innocent, chaste, outraged Lucretia. Pronounce sentence. But if you cannot, because there does not appear any one whom you can punish, why do you extol with such unmeasured laudation her who slew an innocent and chaste woman? Assuredly you will find it impossible to defend her before the judges of the realms below, if they be such as your poets are fond of representing them; for she is among those.

> "Who guiltless sent themselves to doom,
> And all for loathing of the day,
> In madness threw their lives away."

And if she with the others wishes to return,

> "Fate bars the way: around their keep
> The slow unlovely waters creep,
> And bind with ninefold chain."

Or perhaps she is not there, because she slew herself conscious of guilt, not of innocence? She herself alone knows her reason; but what if she was betrayed by the pleasure of the act, and gave some consent to Sextus, though so violently abusing her, and then was so affected with remorse, that she thought death alone could expiate her sin? Even though this were the case, she ought still to have held her hand from suicide, if she could with her false gods have accomplished a fruitful repentance. However, if such were the state of the case, and if it were false that there were two, but one only committed adultery; if the truth were that both were involved in it, one by open assault, the other by secret consent, then she did not kill an innocent woman; and therefore her erudite defenders may maintain that she is not among that class of the dwellers below "who guiltless sent themselves to doom." But this case of Lucretia is in such a dilemma, that if you extenuate the homicide, you confirm the adultery: if you acquit her of adultery, you make the charge of homicide heavier; and there is no way out of the dilemma, when one asks, If she was adulterous, why praise her? if chaste, why slay her?

Nevertheless, for our purpose of refuting those who are unable to comprehend what true sanctity is, and who therefore insult over our outraged Christian women, it is enough that in the instance of this noble Roman matron it was said in her praise, "There were two, but the adultery was the crime of only one." For Lucretia was confidently believed to be superior to the contamination of any consenting thought to the adultery. And accordingly, since she killed herself for being subjected to an outrage in which she had no guilty part, it is obvious that this act of hers was prompted not by the love of purity, but by the overwhelming burden of her shame. She was ashamed that so foul a crime had

been perpetrated upon her, though without her abet-
ting; and this matron, with the Roman love of glory in
her veins, was seized with a proud dread that, if she
continued to live, it would be supposed she willingly
did not resent the wrong that had been done her. She
could not exhibit to men her conscience, but she
judged that her self-inflicted punishment would tes-
tify her state of mind; and she burned with shame at
the thought that her patient endurance of the foul
affront that another had done her, should be con-
strued into complicity with him. Not such was the
decision of the Christian women who suffered as she
did, and yet survive. They declined to avenge upon
themselves the guilt of others, and so add crimes of
their own to those crimes in which they had no share.
For this they would have done had their shame driven
them to homicide, as the lust of their enemies had
driven them to adultery. Within their own souls, in
the witness of their own conscience, they enjoy the
glory of chastity. In the sight of God, too, they are
esteemed pure, and this contents them; they ask no
more: it suffices them to have opportunity of doing
good, and they decline to evade the distress of human
suspicion, lest they thereby deviate from the divine law.

CHAPTER 20

THAT CHRISTIANS HAVE NO AUTHORITY
FOR COMMITTING SUICIDE IN
ANY CIRCUMSTANCES WHATEVER

It is not without significance, that in no passage of the holy canonical books there can be found either divine precept or permission to take away our own life, whether for the sake of entering on the enjoyment of immortality, or of shunning, or ridding ourselves of anything whatever. Nay, the law, rightly interpreted, even prohibits suicide, where it says, "Thou shalt not kill." This is proved especially by the omission of the words "thy neighbor," which are inserted when false witness is forbidden: "Thou shalt not bear false witness against thy neighbor." Nor yet should any one on this account suppose he has not broken this commandment if he has borne false witness only against himself. For the love of our neighbor is regulated by the love of ourselves, as it is written, "Thou shalt love thy neighbor as thyself." If, then, he who makes false statements about himself is not less guilty of bearing false witness than if he had made them to the injury of his neighbor; although in the commandment prohibiting false witness only his neighbor is mentioned, and persons taking no pains to understand it might suppose that a man was allowed to be a false witness to his own hurt; how much greater reason have we to understand that a man may not kill himself, since in the commandment, "Thou shalt not kill," there is no limitation added nor any exception made in favor of any one, and least of all in favor of him on whom the command is laid! And so some attempt to extend this command even to beasts and cattle, as if it forbade us to take life from any creature. But if so, why not extend it also to the plants, and all that is rooted in and nourished by the earth? For though this class of creatures have no sensation, yet they also are said to live, and consequently they can die; and therefore, if violence be done them, can be killed. So, too, the apostle, when speaking of the seeds of such things as these, says, "That which thou sowest is not quickened except it die;" and in the Psalm it is said, "He killed their vines with hail." Must we therefore reckon it a breaking of this commandment, "Thou shalt not kill," to pull a flower? Are we thus insanely to countenance the foolish error of the Manichæans? Putting aside, then, these ravings, if, when we say, Thou shalt not kill, we do not understand this of the plants, since they have no sensation, nor of the irrational animals that fly, swim, walk, or creep, since they are dissociated from us by their want of reason, and are therefore by the just appointment of the Creator subjected to us to kill or keep alive for our own uses; if so, then it remains that we understand that commandment simply of man. The commandment is, "Thou shalt not kill man"; therefore neither another nor yourself, for he who kills himself still kills nothing else than man.

CHAPTER 21

OF THE CASES IN WHICH WE MAY PUT MEN TO DEATH
WITHOUT INCURRING THE GUILT OF MURDER

However, there are some exceptions made by the divine authority to its own law, that men may not be put to death. These exceptions are of two kinds, being justified either by a general law, or by a special commission granted for a time to some individual. And in this latter case, he to whom authority is delegated, and who is but the sword in the hand of him who uses it, is not himself responsible for the death he deals. And, accordingly, they who have waged war in obedience to the divine command, or in conformity with His laws, have represented in their persons the public justice or the wisdom of government, and in this capacity have put to death wicked men; such persons have by no means violated the commandment, "Thou shalt not kill." Abraham indeed was not merely deemed guiltless of cruelty, but was even applauded for his piety, because he was ready to slay his son in obedience to God, not to his own passion. And it is reasonably enough made a question, whether we are to esteem it to have been in compliance with a command of God that Jephthah killed his daughter, because she met him when he had vowed that he would sacrifice to God whatever first met him as he returned victorious from battle. Samson, too, who drew down the house on himself and his foes together, is justified only on this ground, that the Spirit who wrought wonders by him had given him secret instructions to do this. With the exception, then, of these two classes of cases, which are justified either by a just law that applies generally, or by a special intimation from God Himself, the fountain of all justice, whoever kills a man, either himself or another, is implicated in the guilt of murder.

CHAPTER 30

THAT THOSE WHO COMPLAIN OF CHRISTIANITY
REALLY DESIRE TO LIVE WITHOUT RESTRAINT
IN SHAMEFUL LUXURY

If the famous Scipio Nasica were now alive, who was once your pontiff, and was unanimously chosen by the senate, when, in the panic created by the Punic war, they sought for the best citizen to entertain the Phrygian goddess, he would curb this shamelessness of yours, though you would perhaps scarcely dare to look upon the countenance of such a man. For why in your calamities do you complain of Christianity, unless because you desire to enjoy your luxurious license unrestrained, and to lead an abandoned and profligate life without the interruption of any uneasiness or disaster? For certainly your desire for peace, and prosperity, and plenty is not prompted by any purpose of using these blessings honestly, that is to say, with moderation, sobriety, temperance, and piety; for your purpose rather is to run riot in an endless variety of sottish pleasures, and thus to generate from your prosperity a moral pestilence which will prove a thousandfold more disastrous than the fiercest enemies. It was such a calamity as this that Scipio, your chief pontiff, your best man in the judgment of the whole senate, feared when he refused to agree to the destruction of Carthage, Rome's rival; and opposed Cato, who advised its destruction. He feared security, that enemy of weak minds, and he perceived that a wholesome fear would be a fit guardian for the citizens. And he was not mistaken; the event proved how wisely he had spoken. For when Carthage was destroyed, and the Roman republic delivered from its great cause of anxiety, a crowd of disastrous evils forthwith resulted from the prosperous condition of things. First concord was weakened, and destroyed by fierce and bloody seditions; then followed, by a concatenation of baleful causes, civil wars, which brought in their train such massacres, such bloodshed, such lawless and cruel proscription and plunder, that those Romans who, in the days of their virtue, had expected injury only at the hands of their enemies, now that their virtue was lost, suffered greater cruelties at the hands of their fellow-citizens. The lust of rule, which with other vices existed among the Romans in more unmitigated intensity than among any other people, after it had taken possession of the more powerful few, subdued under its yoke the rest, worn and wearied.

CHAPTER 31

BY WHAT STEPS THE PASSION FOR GOVERNING
INCREASED AMONG THE ROMANS

For at what stage would that passion rest when once it has lodged in a proud spirit, until by a succession of advances it has reached even the throne. And to obtain such advances nothing avails but unscrupulous ambition. But unscrupulous ambition has nothing to work upon, save in a nation corrupted by avarice and luxury. Moreover, a people becomes avaricious and luxurious by prosperity; and it was this which that very prudent man Nasica was endeavouring to avoid when he opposed the destruction of the greatest, strongest, wealthiest city of Rome's enemy. He thought that thus fear would act as a curb on lust, and that lust being curbed would not run riot in luxury, and that luxury being prevented avarice would be at an end; and that these vices being banished, virtue would flourish and increase the great profit of the state; and liberty, the fit companion of virtue, would abide unfettered. For similar reasons, and animated by the same considerate patriotism, that same chief pontiff of yours—I still refer to him who was adjudged Rome's best man without one dissentient voice—threw cold water on the proposal of the senate to build a circle of seats round the theatre, and in a very weighty speech warned them against allowing the luxurious manners of Greece to sap the Roman manliness, and persuaded them not to yield to the enervating and emasculating influence of foreign licentiousness. So authoritative and forcible were his words, that the senate was moved to prohibit the use even of those benches which hitherto had been customarily brought to the theatre for the temporary use of the citizens. How eagerly would such a man as this have banished from Rome the scenic exhibitions themselves, had he dared to oppose the authority of those whom he supposed to be gods! For he did not know that they were malicious devils; or if he did, he supposed they should rather be propitiated than despised. For there had not yet been revealed to the Gentiles the heavenly doctrine which should purify their hearts by faith, and transform their natural disposition by humble godliness, and turn them from the service of proud devils to seek the things that are in heaven, or even above the heavens.

CHAPTER 35

OF THE SONS OF THE CHURCH WHO ARE HIDDEN
AMONG THE WICKED, AND OF FALSE CHRISTIANS
WITHIN THE CHURCH

Let these and similar answers (if any fuller and fitter answers can be found) be given to their enemies by the redeemed family of the Lord Christ, and by the pilgrim city of King Christ. But let this city bear in mind, that among her enemies lie hid those who are destined to be fellow-citizens, that she may not think it a fruitless labor to bear what they inflict as enemies until they become confessors of the faith. So, too, as long as she is a stranger in the world, the city of God has in her communion, and bound to her by the sacraments, some who shall not eternally dwell in the lot of the saints. Of these, some are not now recognized; others declare themselves, and do not hesitate to make common cause with our enemies in murmuring against God, whose sacramental badge they wear. These men you may to-day see thronging the churches with us, to-morrow crowding the theatres with the godless. But we have the less reason to despair of the reclamation even of such persons, if among our most declared enemies there are now some, unknown to themselves, who are destined to become our friends. In truth, these two cities are entangled together in this world, and intermixed until the last judgment effects their separation. I now proceed to speak, as God shall help me, of the rise, progress, and end of these two cities; and what I write, I write for the glory of the city of God, that, being placed in comparison with the other, it may shine with a brighter lustre.

BOOK II
CHAPTER 21
CICERO'S OPINION OF THE ROMAN REPUBLIC

But if our adversaries do not care how foully and disgracefully the Roman republic be stained by corrupt practices, so long only as it holds together and continues in being, and if they therefore pooh-pooh the testimony of Sallust to its "utterly wicked and profligate" condition, what will they make of Cicero's statement, that even in his time it had become entirely extinct, and that there remained extant no Roman republic at all? He introduces Scipio (the Scipio who had destroyed Carthage) discussing the republic, at a time when already there were presentiments of its speedy ruin by that corruption which Sallust describes. In fact, at the time when the discussion took place, one of the Gracchi, who, according to Sallust, was the first great instigator of seditions, had already been put to death. His death, indeed, is mentioned in the same book. Now Scipio, at the end of the second book, says: "As among the different sounds which proceed from lyres, flutes, and the human voice, there must be maintained a certain harmony which a cultivated ear cannot endure to hear disturbed or jarring, but which may be elicited in full and absolute concord by the modulation even of voices very unlike one another; so, where reason is allowed to modulate the diverse elements of the state, there is obtained a perfect concord from the upper, lower, and middle classes as from various sounds; and what musicians call harmony in singing, is concord in matters of state, which is the strictest bond and best security of any republic, and which by no ingenuity can be retained where justice has become extinct." Then, when he had expatiated somewhat more fully, and had more copiously illustrated the benefits of its presence and the ruinous effects of its absence upon a state, Pilus, one of the company present at the discussion, struck in and demanded that the question should be more thoroughly sifted, and that the subject of justice should be freely discussed for the sake of ascertaining what truth there was in the maxim which was then becoming daily more current, that "the republic cannot be governed without injustice." Scipio expressed his willingness to have this maxim discussed and sifted, and gave it as his opinion that it was baseless, and that no progress could be made in discussing the republic unless it was established, not only that this maxim, that "the republic cannot be governed without injustice," was false, but also that the truth is, that it cannot be governed without the most absolute justice. And the discussion of this question, being deferred till the next day, is carried on in the third book with great animation. For Pilus himself undertook to defend the position that the republic cannot be governed without injustice, at the same time being at special pains to clear himself of any real participation in that opinion. He advocated with great keenness the cause of injustice against justice, and endeavored by plausible reasons and examples to demonstrate that the former is beneficial, the latter useless, to the republic. Then, at the request of the company, Lælius attempted to defend justice, and strained every nerve to prove that nothing is so hurtful to a state as injustice; and that without justice a republic can neither be governed, nor even continue to exist.

When this question has been handled to the satisfaction of the company, Scipio reverts to the original thread of discourse, and repeats with commendation his own brief definition of a republic, that it is the weal of the people. "The people," he defines as being not every assemblage or mob, but an assemblage associated by a common acknowledgment of law, and by a community of interests. Then he shows the use of definition in debate; and from these definitions of his own he gathers that a republic, or "weal of the people," then exists only when it is well and justly governed, whether by a monarch, or an aristocracy, or by the whole people. But when the monarch is unjust, or, as the Greeks say, a tyrant; or the aristocrats are unjust, and form a faction; or the people themselves are unjust, and become, as Scipio for want of a better name calls them, themselves the tyrant, then the republic is not only blemished (as had been proved the day before), but by legitimate deduction from those definitions, it altogether ceases to be. For it could not be the people's weal when a tyrant factiously lorded it over the state; neither would the people be any longer a people if it were unjust, since it would no longer answer the definition of a people—"an assemblage associated by a common acknowledgment of law, and by a community of interests."

When, therefore, the Roman republic was such as Sallust described it, it was not "utterly wicked and profligate," as he says, but had altogether ceased to exist, if we are to admit the reasoning of that debate maintained on the subject of the republic by its best representatives. Tully himself, too, speaking not in the person of Scipio or any one else, but uttering his own sentiments, uses the following language in the beginning of the fifth book, after quoting a line from the poet Ennius, in which he said, "Rome's severe morality and her citizens are her safeguard." "This verse," says Cicero, "seems to me to have all the sententious truthfulness of an oracle. For neither would the citizens have availed without the morality of the community, nor would the morality of the commons without outstanding men have availed either to establish or so long to maintain in vigor so grand a republic with so wide and just an empire. Accordingly, before our day, the hereditary usages formed our foremost men, and they on their part retained the usages and institutions of their fathers. But our age, receiving the republic as a chef-d'oeuvre of another age which has already begun to grow old, has not merely neglected to restore the colors of the original, but has not even been at the pains to preserve so much as the general outline and most outstanding features. For what survives of that primitive morality which the poet called Rome's safeguard? It is so obsolete and forgotten, that, far from practising it, one does not even know it. And of the citizens what shall I say? Morality has perished through poverty of great men; a poverty for which we must not only assign a reason, but for the guilt of which we must answer as criminals charged with a capital crime. For it is through our vices, and not by any mishap, that we retain only the name of a republic, and have long since lost the reality."

This is the confession of Cicero, long indeed after the death of Africanus, whom he introduced as an interlocutor in his work *De Republica*, but still before the coming of Christ. Yet, if the disasters he bewails had been lamented after the Christian religion had been diffused, and had begun to prevail, is there a man of our adversaries who would not have thought that they were to be imputed to the Christians? Why, then, did their gods not take steps then to prevent the decay and extinction of that republic, over the loss of which Cicero, long before Christ had come in the flesh, sings so lugubrious a dirge? Its admirers have need to inquire whether, even in the days of primitive men and morals, true justice flourished in it; or was it not perhaps even then, to use the casual expression of Cicero, rather a colored painting than the living reality? But, if God will, we shall consider this elsewhere. For I mean in its own place to show that—according to the definitions in which Cicero himself, using Scipio as his mouthpiece, briefly propounded what a republic is, and what a people is, and according to many testimonies, both of his own lips and of those who took part in that same debate— Rome never was a republic, because true justice had never a place in it. But accepting the more feasible definitions of a republic, I grant there was a republic of a certain kind, and certainly much better administered by the more ancient Romans than by their modern representatives. But the fact is, true justice has no existence save in that republic whose founder and ruler is Christ, if at least any choose to call this a republic; and indeed we cannot deny that it is the people's weal. But if perchance this name, which has become familiar in other

connections, be considered alien to our common par-
lance, we may at all events say that in this city is true
justice; the city of which Holy Scripture says, "Glorious
things are said of thee, O city of God."

BOOK IV

CHAPTER 3

WHETHER THE GREAT EXTENT OF THE EMPIRE,

WHICH HAS BEEN ACQUIRED ONLY BY WARS, IS

TO BE RECKONED AMONG THE GOOD THINGS EITHER

OF THE WISE OR THE HAPPY

Now, therefore, let us see how it is that they dare to
ascribe the very great extent and duration of the Roman
empire to those gods whom they contend that they worship honorably, even by the obsequies of vile games and
the ministry of vile men: although I should like first to
inquire for a little what reason, what prudence, there is
in wishing to glory in the greatness and extent of the
empire, when you cannot point out the happiness of
men who are always rolling, with dark fear and cruel
lust, in warlike slaughters and in blood, which, whether
shed in civil or foreign war, is still human blood; so that
their joy may be compared to glass in its fragile splen-
dor, of which one is horribly afraid lest it should be
suddenly broken in pieces. That this may be more easily
discerned, let us not come to nought by being carried
away with empty boasting, or blunt the edge of our

attention by loud-sounding names of things, when we
hear of peoples, kingdoms, provinces. But let us suppose
a case of two men; for each individual man, like one
letter in a language, is as it were the element of a city or
kingdom, however far-spreading in its occupation of
the earth. Of these two men let us suppose that one is
poor, or rather of middling circumstances; the other
very rich. But the rich man is anxious with fears, pining
with discontent, burning with covetousness, never
secure, always uneasy, panting from the perpetual strife
of his enemies, adding to his patrimony indeed by these
miseries to an immense degree, and by these additions
also heaping up most bitter cares. But that other man of
moderate wealth is contented with a small and compact
estate, most dear to his own family, enjoying the sweet-
est peace with his kindred neighbors and friends, in
piety religious, benignant in mind, healthy in body, in
life frugal, in manners chaste, in conscience secure. I
know not whether any one can be such a fool, that he
dare hesitate which to prefer. As, therefore, in the case
of these two men, so in two families, in two nations, in
two kingdoms, this test of tranquility holds good; and
if we apply it vigilantly and without prejudice, we shall
quite easily see where the mere show of happiness
dwells, and where real felicity. Wherefore if the true
God is worshipped, and if He is served with genuine
rites and true virtue, it is advantageous that good men

should long reign both far and wide. Nor is this advantageous so much to themselves, as to those over whom they reign. For, so far as concerns themselves, their piety and probity, which are great gifts of God, suffice to give them true felicity, enabling them to live well the life that now is, and afterwards to receive that which is eternal. In this world, therefore, the dominion of good men is profitable, not so much for themselves as for human affairs. But the dominion of bad men is hurtful chiefly to themselves who rule, for they destroy their own souls by greater license in wickedness; while those who are put under them in service are not hurt except by their own iniquity. For to the just all the evils imposed on them by unjust rulers are not the punishment of crime, but the test of virtue. Therefore the good man, although he is a slave, is free; but the bad man, even if he reigns, is a slave, and that not of one man, but, what is far more grievous, of as many masters as he has vices; of which vices when the divine Scripture treats, it says, "For of whom any man is overcome, to the same he is also the bond-slave."

CHAPTER 4

HOW LIKE KINGDOMS WITHOUT JUSTICE

ARE TO ROBBERIES

Justice being taken away, then, what are kingdoms but great robberies? For what are robberies themselves, but little kingdoms? The band itself is made up of men; it is ruled by the authority of a prince, it is knit together by the pact of the confederacy; the booty is divided by the law agreed on. If, by the admittance of abandoned men, this evil increases to such a degree that it holds places, fixes abodes, takes possession of cities, and subdues peoples, it assumes the more plainly the name of a kingdom, because the reality is now manifestly conferred on it, not by the removal of covetousness, but by the addition of impunity. Indeed, that was an apt and true reply which was given to Alexander the Great by a pirate who had been seized. For when that king had asked the man what he meant by keeping hostile possession of the sea, he answered with bold pride, "What thou meanest by seizing the whole earth; but because I do it with a petty ship, I am called a robber, whilst thou who dost it with a great fleet art styled emperor."

CHAPTER 33

THAT THE TIMES OF ALL KINGS AND KINGDOMS
ARE ORDAINED BY THE JUDGMENT AND
POWER OF THE TRUE GOD

Therefore that God, the author and giver of felicity, because He alone is the true God, Himself gives earthly kingdoms both to good and bad. Neither does He do this rashly, and, as it were, fortuitously—because He is God not fortune—but according to the order of things and times, which is hidden from us, but thoroughly known to Himself; which same order of times, however, He does not serve as subject to it, but Himself rules as lord and appoints as governor. Felicity He gives only to the good. Whether a man be a subject or a king makes no difference; he may equally either possess or not possess it. And it shall be full in that life where kings and subjects exist no longer. And therefore earthly kingdoms are given by Him both to the good and the bad; lest His worshippers, still under the conduct of a very weak mind, should covet these gifts from Him as some great things. And this is the mystery of the Old Testament, in which the New was hidden, that there even earthly gifts are promised: those who were spiritual understanding even then, although not yet openly declaring, both the eternity which was symbolized by these earthly things, and in what gifts of God true felicity could be found.

BOOK V

CHAPTER 15

CONCERNING THE TEMPORAL REWARD WHICH
GOD GRANTED TO THE VIRTUES OF THE ROMANS

Now, therefore, with regard to those to whom God did not purpose to give eternal life with His holy angels in His own celestial city, to the society of which that true piety which does not render the service of religion, which

the Greeks call λατρεία, to any save the true God con-
ducts, if He had also withheld from them the terrestrial
glory of that most excellent empire, a reward would not
have been rendered to their good arts—that is, their
virtues—by which they sought to attain so great glory.
For as to those who seem to do some good that they
may receive glory from men, the Lord also says, "Verily
I say unto you, they have received their reward." So also
these despised their own private affairs for the sake of the
republic, and for its treasury resisted avarice, consulted
for the good of their country with a spirit of freedom,
addicted neither to what their laws pronounced to be
crime nor to lust. By all these acts, as by the true way, they
pressed forward to honors, power, and glory; they were
honored among almost all nations; they imposed the laws
of their empire upon many nations; and at this day, both
in literature and history, they are glorious among almost
all nations. There is no reason why they should complain
against the justice of the supreme and true God—"they
have received their reward."

CHAPTER 16

CONCERNING THE REWARD OF THE HOLY CITIZENS OF
THE CELESTIAL CITY, TO WHOM THE EXAMPLE OF THE
VIRTUES OF THE ROMANS ARE USEFUL

But the reward of the saints is far different, who even
here endured reproaches for that city of God which is

hateful to the lovers of this world. That city is eternal.
There none are born, for none die. There is true and
full felicity—not a goddess, but a gift of God. Thence
we receive the pledge of faith, whilst on our pilgrimage
we sigh for its beauty. There rises not the sun on the
good and the evil, but the Sun of Righteousness protects the good alone. There no great industry shall be
expended to enrich the public treasury by suffering pri-
vations at home, for there is the common treasury of
truth. And, therefore, it was not only for the sake of
recompensing the citizens of Rome that her empire and
glory had been so signally extended, but also that the
citizens of that eternal city, during their pilgrimage
here, might diligently and soberly contemplate these
examples, and see what a love they owe to the supernal
country on account of life eternal, if the terrestrial
country was so much beloved by its citizens on account
of human glory.

CHAPTER 17

TO WHAT PROFIT THE ROMANS CARRIED ON WARS, AND
HOW MUCH THEY CONTRIBUTED TO THE WELL-BEING
OF THOSE WHOM THEY CONQUERED

For, as far as this life of mortals is concerned, which is
spent and ended in a few days, what does it matter
under whose government a dying man lives, if they who
govern do not force him to impiety and iniquity? Did

the Romans at all harm those nations, on whom, when
subjugated, they imposed their laws, except in as far as
that was accomplished with great slaughter in war?
Now, had it been done with consent of the nations, it
would have been done with greater success, but there
would have been no glory of conquest, for neither did
the Romans themselves live exempt from those laws
which they imposed on others. Had this been done
without Mars and Bellona, so that there should have
been no place for victory, no one conquering where no
one had fought, would not the condition of the Romans
and of the other nations have been one and the same,
especially if that had been done at once which afterwards was done most humanely and most acceptably,
namely, the admission of all to the rights of Roman
citizens who belonged to the Roman empire, and if that
had been made the privilege of all which was formerly
the privilege of a few, with this one condition, that the
humbler class who had no lands of their own should
live at the public expense—an alimentary impost,
which would have been paid with a much better grace
by them into the hands of good administrators of the
republic, of which they were members, by their own
hearty consent, than it would have been paid with had
it to be extorted from them as conquered men? For I do
not see what it makes for the safety, good morals, and
certainly not for the dignity, of men, that some have

conquered and others have been conquered, except that it yields them that most insane pomp of human glory, in which "they have received their reward," who burned with excessive desire of it, and carried on most eager wars. For do not their lands pay tribute? Have they any privilege of learning what the others are not privileged to learn? Are there not many senators in the other countries who do not even know Rome by sight? Take away outward show, and what are all men after all but men? But even though the perversity of the age should permit that all the better men should be more highly honored than others, neither thus should human honor be held at a great price, for it is smoke which has no weight. But let us avail ourselves even in these things of the kindness of God. Let us consider how great things they despised, how great things they endured, what lusts they subdued for the sake of human glory, who merited that glory, as it were, in reward for such virtues; and let this be useful to us even in suppressing pride, so that, as that city in which it has been promised us to reign as far surpasses this one as heaven is distant from the earth, as eternal life surpasses temporal joy, solid glory empty praise, or the society of angels the society of mortals, or the glory of Him who made the sun and moon the light of the sun and moon, the citizens of so great a country may not seem to themselves to have done anything very great, if, in order to obtain it, they have done some good works or endured some evils, when those men for this terrestrial country already obtained, did such great things, suffered such great things. And especially are all these things to be considered, because the remission of sins which collects citizens to the celestial country has something in it to which a shadowy resemblance is found in that asylum of Romulus, whither escape from the punishment of all manner of crimes congregated that multitude with which the state was to be founded.

CHAPTER 19

CONCERNING THE DIFFERENCE BETWEEN TRUE
GLORY AND THE DESIRE OF DOMINATION

There is assuredly a difference between the desire of human glory and the desire of domination; for, though he who has an overweening delight in human glory will be also very prone to aspire earnestly after domination, nevertheless they who desire the true glory even of human praise strive not to displease those who judge well of them. For there are many good moral qualities, of which many are competent judges, although they are not possessed by many; and by those good moral qualities those men press on to glory, honor and domination, of whom Sallust says, "But they press on by the true way."

But whosoever, without possessing that desire of glory which makes one fear to displease those who judge his conduct, desires domination and power, very often seeks to obtain what he loves by most open crimes. Therefore he who desires glory presses on to obtain it either by the true way, or certainly by deceit and artifice, wishing to appear good when he is not. Therefore to him who possesses virtues it is a great virtue to despise glory; for contempt of it is seen by God, but is not manifest to human judgment. For whatever any one does before the eyes of men in order to show himself to be a despiser of glory, if they suspect that he is doing it in order to get greater praise—that is, greater glory—he has no means of demonstrating to the perceptions of those who suspect him that the case is really otherwise than they suspect it to be. But he who despises the judgment of praisers, despises also the rashness of suspectors. Their salvation, indeed, he does not despise, if he is truly good; for so great is the righteousness of that man who receives his virtues from the Spirit of God, that he loves his very enemies, and so loves them that he desires that his haters and detractors may be turned to righteousness, and become his associates, and that not in an earthly but in a heavenly country. But with respect to his praisers, though he sets little value on their praise, he does not set little value on their love; neither does he elude their praise, lest he should forfeit their love. And, therefore, he strives earnestly to have their praises directed to Him from whom every one receives whatever in him is truly praiseworthy. But he who is a

despiser of glory, but is greedy of domination, exceeds
the beasts in the vices of cruelty and luxuriousness.
Such, indeed, were certain of the Romans, who, wanting the love of esteem, wanted not the thirst for domination; and that there were many such, history testifies.
But it was Nero Cæsar who was the first to reach the
summit, and, as it were, the citadel, of this vice; for so
great was his luxuriousness, that one would have thought
there was nothing manly to be dreaded in him, and
such his cruelty, that, had not the contrary been known,
no one would have thought there was anything effemi-
nate in his character. Nevertheless power and domination are not given even to such men save by the providence
of the most high God, when He judges that the state of
human affairs is worthy of such lords. The divine utter-
ance is clear on this matter; for the Wisdom of God
thus speaks: "By me kings reign, and tyrants possess the
land." But, that it may not be thought that by "tyrants"
is meant, not wicked and impious kings, but brave men,
in accordance with the ancient use of the word, as when
Virgil says,

"For know that treaty may not stand
Where king greets king and joins not hand,"

in another place it is most unambiguously said of God,
that He "maketh the man who is an hypocrite to reign

on account of the perversity of the people." Wherefore, though I have, according to my ability, shown for what reason God, who alone is true and just, helped forward the Romans, who were good according to a certain standard of an earthly state, to the acquirement of the glory of so great an empire, there may be, nevertheless, a more hidden cause, known better to God than to us, depending on the diversity of the merits of the human race. Among all who are truly pious, it is at all events agreed that no one without true piety—that is, true worship of the true God—can have true virtue; and that it is not true virtue which is the slave of human praise. Though, nevertheless, they who are not citizens of the eternal city, which is called the city of God in the sacred Scriptures, are more useful to the earthly city when they possess even that virtue than if they had not even that. But there could be nothing more fortunate for human affairs than that, by the mercy of God, they who are endowed with true piety of life, if they have the skill for ruling people, should also have the power. But such men, however great virtues they may possess in this life, attribute it solely to the grace of God that He has bestowed it on them—willing, believing, seeking. And, at the same time, they understand how far they are short of that perfection of righteousness which exists in the society of those holy angels for which they are striving to fit themselves. But however much that virtue may be praised and cried up, which without true piety is the slave of human glory, it is not at all to be compared even to the feeble beginnings of the virtue of the saints, whose hope is placed in the grace and mercy of the true God.

BOOK XIV

CHAPTER 28

OF THE NATURE OF THE TWO CITIES,

THE EARTHLY AND THE HEAVENLY

Accordingly, two cities have been formed by two loves: the earthly by the love of self, even to the contempt of God; the heavenly by the love of God, even to the contempt of self. The former, in a word, glories in itself, the latter in the Lord. For the one seeks glory from men; but the greatest glory of the other is God, the witness of conscience. The one lifts up its head in its own glory; the other says to its God, "Thou art my glory, and the lifter up of mine head." In the one, the princes and the nations it subdues are ruled by the love of ruling; in the other, the princes and the subjects serve one another in love, the latter obeying, while the former take thought for all. The one delights in its own strength, represented in the persons of its rulers; the other says to its God, "I will love Thee, O Lord, my strength." Therefore the wise men of the one city, living according to man, have sought for profit to their own bodies or souls, or both, and those who have known God "glorified Him not as God, neither were thankful, but became vain in their imaginations, and their foolish heart was darkened; professing themselves to be wise"—that is, glorying in their own wisdom, and being possessed by pride—"they became fools, and changed the glory of the incorruptible God into an image made like to corruptible man, and to birds, and four-footed beasts, and creeping things." For they were either leaders or followers of the people in adoring images, "and worshipped and served the creature more than the Creator, who is blessed for ever." But in the other city there is no human wisdom, but only godliness, which offers due worship to the true God, and looks for its reward in the society of the saints, of holy angels as well as holy men, "that God may be all in all."

BOOK XV

CHAPTER 4

OF THE CONFLICT AND PEACE OF THE EARTHLY CITY

But the earthly city, which shall not be everlasting (for it will no longer be a city when it has been committed to the extreme penalty), has its good in this world, and rejoices in it with such joy as such things can afford. But as this is not a good which can discharge its devotees of all distresses, this city is often divided against itself by litigations, wars, quarrels, and such victories as are either life-destroying or short-lived. For each part of it that arms against another part of it seeks to triumph over the nations through itself in bondage to vice. If, when it has conquered, it is inflated with pride, its victory is life-destroying; but if it turns its thoughts upon the common casualties of our mortal condition, and is rather anxious concerning the disasters that may befall it than elated with the successes already achieved, this victory, though of a higher kind, is still only short-lived; for it cannot abidingly rule over those whom it has victoriously subjugated. But the things which this city desires cannot justly be said to be evil, for it is itself, in its own kind, better than all other human good. For it desires earthly peace for the sake of enjoying earthly goods, and it makes war in order to attain to this peace; since, if it has conquered, and there remains no one to resist it, it enjoys a peace which it had not while there were opposing parties who contested for the enjoyment of those things which were too small to satisfy both. This peace is purchased by toilsome wars; it is obtained by what they style a glorious victory. Now, when victory remains with the party which had the juster cause, who hesitates to congratulate the victor, and style it a desirable peace? These things, then, are good things, and without doubt the gifts of God. But if they neglect the better things of the heavenly city, which are secured by eternal victory and peace never-ending, and so inordinately covet these present good things that they believe them to be the only desirable things, or love them better than those things which are believed to be better—if this be so, then it is necessary that misery follow and ever increase.

CHAPTER 5

OF THE FRATRICIDAL ACT OF THE FOUNDER
OF THE EARTHLY CITY, AND THE CORRESPONDING
CRIME OF THE FOUNDER OF ROME

Thus the founder of the earthly city was a fratricide. Overcome with envy, he slew his own brother, a citizen of the eternal city, and a sojourner on earth. So that we cannot be surprised that this first specimen, or, as the Greeks say, archetype of crime, should, long afterwards, find a corresponding crime at the foundation of that city which was destined to reign over so many nations, and be the head of this earthly city of which we speak. For of that city also, as one of their poets has mentioned, "the first walls were stained with a brother's blood," or, as Roman history records, Remus was slain by his brother Romulus. And thus there is no difference between the foundation of this city and of the earthly city, unless it be that Romulus and Remus were both citizens of the earthly city. Both desired to have the glory of founding the Roman republic, but both could not have as much glory as if one only

claimed it; for he who wished to have the glory of ruling would certainly rule less if his power were shared
by a living consort. In order, therefore, that the whole
glory might be enjoyed by one, his consort was removed;
and by this crime the empire was made larger indeed,
but inferior, while otherwise it would have been less,
but better. Now these brothers, Cain and Abel, were
not both animated by the same earthly desires, nor did
the murderer envy the other because he feared that, by
both ruling, his own dominion would be curtailed—
for Abel was not solicitous to rule in that city which
his brother built—he was moved by that diabolical,
envious hatred with which the evil regard the good, for
no other reason than because they are good while
themselves are evil. For the possession of goodness is
by no means diminished by being shared with a partner either permanent or temporarily assumed; on the
contrary, the possession of goodness is increased in
proportion to the concord and charity of each of those
who share it. In short, he who is unwilling to share this
possession cannot have it; and he who is most willing
to admit others to a share of it will have the greatest
abundance to himself. The quarrel, then, between
Romulus and Remus shows how the earthly city is
divided against itself; that which fell out between Cain
and Abel illustrated the hatred that subsists between
the two cities, that of God and that of men. The wicked

war with the wicked; the good also war with the wicked. But with the good, good men, or at least perfectly good men, cannot war; though, while only going on towards perfection, they war to this extent, that every good man resists others in those points in which he resists himself. And in each individual "the flesh lusteth against the spirit, and the spirit against the flesh." This spiritual lusting, therefore, can be at war with the carnal lust of another man; or carnal lust may be at war with the spiritual desires of another, in some such way as good and wicked men are at war; or, still more certainly, the carnal lusts of two men, good but not yet perfect, contend together, just as the wicked contend with the wicked, until the health of those who are under the treatment of grace attains final victory.

CHAPTER 6

OF THE WEAKNESSES WHICH EVEN THE CITIZENS
OF THE CITY OF GOD SUFFER DURING THIS EARTHLY
PILGRIMAGE IN PUNISHMENT OF SIN, AND OF WHICH
THEY ARE HEALED BY GOD'S CARE

This sickliness—that is to say, that disobedience of which we spoke in the fourteenth book—is the punishment of the first disobedience. It is therefore not nature, but vice; and therefore it is said to the good who are growing in grace, and living in this pilgrimage by faith, "Bear ye one another's burdens, and so fulfill the law of

Christ." In like manner it is said elsewhere, "Warn them that are unruly, comfort the feeble-minded, support the weak, be patient toward all men. See that none render evil for evil unto any man." And in another place, "If a man be overtaken in a fault, ye which are spiritual restore such an one in the spirit of meekness; considering thyself, lest thou also be tempted." And elsewhere, "Let not the sun go down upon your wrath." And in the Gospel, "If thy brother shall trespass against thee, go and tell him his fault between thee and him alone." So too of sins which may create scandal the apostle says, "Them that sin rebuke before all, that others also may fear." For this purpose, and that we may keep that peace without which no man can see the Lord, many precepts are given which carefully inculcate mutual forgiveness; among which we may number that terrible word in which the servant is ordered to pay his formerly remitted debt of ten thousand talents, because he did not remit to his fellow-servant his debt of two hundred pence. To which parable the Lord Jesus added the words, "So likewise shall my heavenly Father do also unto you, if ye from your hearts forgive not every one his brother." It is thus the citizens of the city of God are healed while still they sojourn in this earth and sigh for the peace of their heavenly country. The Holy Spirit, too, works within, that the medicine externally applied may have some good result. Otherwise, even though God Himself make use of the creatures that are subject to Him, and in some human form address our human senses, whether we receive those impressions in sleep or in some external appearance, still, if He does not by His own inward grace sway and act upon the mind, no preaching of the truth is of any avail. But this God does, distinguishing between the vessels of wrath and the vessels of mercy, by His own very secret but very just providence. When He Himself aids the soul in His own hidden and wonderful ways, and the sin which dwells in our members, and is, as the apostle teaches, rather the punishment of sin, does not reign in our mortal body to obey the lusts of it, and when we no longer yield our members as instruments of unrighteousness, then the soul is converted from its own evil and selfish desires, and, God possessing it, it possesses itself in peace even in this life, and afterwards, with perfected health and endowed with immortality, will reign without sin in peace everlasting.

Augustine's project defies rapid summary, but he himself, while often acknowledging in passing that he has let himself be sidetracked by the need to refute an opponent or develop a point that readers have found confusing, preserved a sense of the overall scheme of the work; it was to be a universal history, embracing the fate of the two cities.

BOOK XVIII

CHAPTER I

OF THOSE THINGS DOWN TO THE TIMES OF
THE SAVIOUR WHICH HAVE BEEN DISCUSSED
IN THE SEVENTEEN BOOKS

I promised to write of the rise, progress, and appointed end of the two cities, one of which is God's, the other this world's, in which, so far as mankind is concerned, the former is now a stranger. But first of all I undertook, so far as His grace should enable me, to refute the enemies of the city of God, who prefer their gods to Christ its founder, and fiercely hate Christians with the most deadly malice. And this I have done in the first ten books. Then, as regards my three-fold promise which I have just mentioned, I have treated distinctly, in the four books which follow the tenth, of the rise of both cities. After that, I have proceeded from the first man down to the flood in one book, which is the fifteenth of this work; and from that again down to Abraham our work has followed both in chronological order. From the patriarch Abraham down to the time of the Israelite kings, at which we close our sixteenth book, and thence down to the advent of Christ Himself in the flesh, to which period the seventeenth book reaches, the city of God appears from my way of writing to have run its course alone; whereas it did not run its course alone in this age, for both cities, in their course amid mankind, certainly experienced chequered times together just as from the beginning. But I did this in order that, first of all, from the time when the promises of God began to be more clear, down to the virgin birth of Him in whom those things promised from the first were to be fulfilled, the course of that city which is God's might be made more distinctly apparent, without interpolation of foreign matter from the history of the other city, although down to the revelation of the new covenant it ran its course, not in light, but in shadow. Now, therefore, I think fit to do what I passed by, and show, so far as seems necessary, how that other city ran its course from the times of Abraham, so that attentive readers may compare the two.

CHAPTER 49

OF THE INDISCRIMINATE INCREASE OF THE CHURCH, WHEREIN MANY REPROBATE ARE IN THIS WORLD MIXED WITH THE ELECT

In this wicked world, in these evil days, when the Church measures her future loftiness by her present humility, and is exercised by goading fears, tormenting sorrows, disquieting labors, and dangerous temptations, when she soberly rejoices, rejoicing only in hope, there are many reprobate mingled with the good, and both are gathered together by the gospel as in a drag net; and in this world, as in a sea, both swim enclosed without distinction in the net, until it is brought ashore, when the wicked must be separated from the good, that in the good, as in His temple, God may be all in all. We acknowledge, indeed, that His word is now fulfilled who spake in the psalm, and said, "I have announced and spoken; they are multiplied above number." This takes place now, since He has spoken, first by the mouth of his forerunner John, and afterward by His own mouth, saying, "Repent: for the kingdom of heaven is at hand." He chose disciples, whom He also called apostles, of lowly birth, unhonored, and illiterate, so that whatever great thing they might be or do, He might be and do it in them. He had one among them whose wickedness He could use well in order to accomplish His appointed passion, and furnish His Church an example of bearing with the wicked. Having sown the holy gospel as much as that behoved to be done by His bodily presence, He suffered, died, and rose again, showing by His passion what we ought to suffer for the truth, and by His resurrection what we ought to hope for in adversity; saving always the mystery of the sacrament, by which His blood was shed for the remission of sins. He held converse on the earth forty days with His disciples, and in their sight ascended into heaven, and after ten days sent the promised Holy Spirit. It was given as the chief and most necessary sign of His coming on those who had believed, that every one of them spoke in the tongues of all nations; thus signifying that the unity of the catholic Church would embrace all nations, and would in like manner speak in all tongues.

BOOK XIX

Augustine returns to the goals and achievements of the two cities, beginning from the contrast between pagan and Christian conceptions of the ultimate ends of life—"the supreme good." His discussion of the 288 sects distinguished by Varro is minute; but his aim is to defend the Christian ideal, and to refute the claim that the supreme good can be attained in this life, even by the most self-controlled philosopher. It is in book 19 that many of Augustine's observations on political morality occur.

CHAPTER 4

WHAT THE CHRISTIANS BELIEVE REGARDING
THE SUPREME GOOD AND EVIL, IN OPPOSITION
TO THE PHILOSOPHERS, WHO HAVE MAINTAINED THAT
THE SUPREME GOOD IS IN THEMSELVES

If, then, we be asked what the city of God has to say upon these points, and, in the first place, what its opinion regarding the supreme good and evil is, it will reply that life eternal is the supreme good, death eternal the supreme evil, and that to obtain the one and escape the other we must live rightly. And thus it is written, "The just lives by

faith," for we do not as yet see our good, and must therefore live by faith; neither have we in ourselves power to
live rightly, but can do so only if He who has given us
faith to believe in His help do help us when we believe
and pray. As for those who have supposed that the sovereign good and evil are to be found in this life, and have
placed it either in the soul or the body, or in both, or, to
speak more explicitly, either in pleasure or in virtue, or
in both; in repose or in virtue, or in both; in pleasure
and repose, or in virtue, or in all combined; in the primary objects of nature, or in virtue, or in both—all
these have, with a marvelous shallowness, sought to
find their blessedness in this life and in themselves.
Contempt has been poured upon such ideas by the
Truth, saying by the prophet, "The Lord knoweth the
thoughts of men" (or, as the Apostle Paul cites the
passage, "The Lord knoweth the thoughts of the
wise") "that they are vain."

For what flood of eloquence can suffice to detail the
miseries of this life? Cicero, in the Consolation on the
death of his daughter, has spent all his ability in lamen-
tation; but how inadequate was even his ability here?
For when, where, how, in this life can these primary
objects of nature be possessed so that they may not be
assailed by unforeseen accidents? Is the body of the wise
man exempt from any pain which may dispel pleasure,
from any disquietude which may banish repose? The

amputation or decay of the members of the body puts an end to its integrity, deformity blights its beauty, weakness its health, lassitude its vigor, sleepiness or sluggishness its activity—and which of these is it that may not assail the flesh of the wise man? Comely and fitting attitudes and movements of the body are numbered among the prime natural blessings; but what if some sickness makes the members tremble? what if a man suffers from curvature of the spine to such an extent that his hands reach the ground, and he goes upon all-fours like a quadruped? Does not this destroy all beauty and grace in the body, whether at rest or in motion? What shall I say of the fundamental blessings of the soul, sense and intellect, of which the one is given for the perception, and the other for the comprehension of truth? But what kind of sense is it that remains when a man becomes deaf and blind? where are reason and intellect when disease makes a man delirious? We can scarcely, or not at all, refrain from tears, when we think of or see the actions and words of such frantic persons, and consider how different from and even opposed to their own sober judgment and ordinary conduct their present demeanor is. And what shall I say of those who suffer from demoniacal possession? Where is their own intelligence hidden and buried while the malignant spirit is using their body and soul according to his own will? And who is quite sure that no such thing can hap-

pen to the wise man in this life? Then, as to the perception of truth, what can we hope for even in this way
while in the body, as we read in the true book of Wisdom, "The corruptible body weigheth down the soul,
and the earthly tabernacle presseth down the mind that
museth upon many things?" And eagerness, or desire of
action, if this is the right meaning to put upon the
Greek ὁρμή, is also reckoned among the primary advantages of nature; and yet is it not this which produces
those pitiable movements of the insane, and those
actions which we shudder to see, when sense is deceived
and reason deranged?

In fine, virtue itself, which is not among the primary objects of nature, but succeeds to them as the
result of learning, though it holds the highest place
among human good things, what is its occupation save
to wage perpetual war with vices—not those that are
outside of us, but within; not other men's, but our
own—a war which is waged especially by that virtue
which the Greeks call σωφροσύνη, and we temperance,
and which bridles carnal lusts, and prevents them from
winning the consent of the spirit to wicked deeds? For
we must not fancy that there is no vice in us, when, as
the apostle says, "The flesh lusteth against the spirit";
for to this vice there is a contrary virtue, when, as the
same writer says, "The spirit lusteth against the flesh."
"For these two," he says, "are contrary one to the other,

so that you cannot do the things which you would." But what is it we wish to do when we seek to attain the supreme good, unless that the flesh should cease to lust against the spirit, and that there be no vice in us against which the spirit may lust? And as we cannot attain to this in the present life, however ardently we desire it, let us by God's help accomplish at least this, to preserve the soul from succumbing and yielding to the flesh that lusts against it, and to refuse our consent to the perpetration of sin. Far be it from us, then, to fancy that while we are still engaged in this intestine war, we have already found the happiness which we seek to reach by victory. And who is there so wise that he has no conflict at all to maintain against his vices?

What shall I say of that virtue which is called prudence? Is not all its vigilance spent in the discernment of good from evil things, so that no mistake may be admitted about what we should desire and what avoid? And thus it is itself a proof that we are in the midst of evils, or that evils are in us; for it teaches us that it is an evil to consent to sin, and a good to refuse this consent. And yet this evil, to which prudence teaches and temperance enables us not to consent, is removed from this life neither by prudence nor by temperance. And justice, whose office it is to render to every man his due, whereby there is in man himself a certain just order of nature, so that the soul is subjected to God, and the flesh to the

soul, and consequently both soul and flesh to God—
does not this virtue demonstrate that it is as yet rather
laboring towards its end than resting in its finished
work? For the soul is so much the less subjected to God
as it is less occupied with the thought of God; and the
flesh is so much the less subjected to the spirit as it lusts
more vehemently against the spirit. So long, therefore,
as we are beset by this weakness, this plague, this disease, how shall we dare to say that we are safe? and if
not safe, then how can we be already enjoying our final
beatitude? Then that virtue which goes by the name of
fortitude is the plainest proof of the ills of life, for it is
these ills which it is compelled to bear patiently. And
this holds good, no matter though the ripest wisdom
co-exists with it. And I am at a loss to understand how
the Stoic philosophers can presume to say that these are
no ills, though at the same time they allow the wise man
to commit suicide and pass out of this life if they
become so grievous that he cannot or ought not to
endure them. But such is the stupid pride of these men
who fancy that the supreme good can be found in this
life, and that they can become happy by their own
resources, that their wise man, or at least the man whom
they fancifully depict as such, is always happy, even
though he become blind, deaf, dumb, mutilated, racked
with pains, or suffer any conceivable calamity such as
may compel him to make away with himself; and they

are not ashamed to call the life that is beset with these evils happy. O happy life, which seeks the aid of death to end it? If it is happy, let the wise man remain in it; but if these ills drive him out of it, in what sense is it happy? Or how can they say that these are not evils which conquer the virtue of fortitude, and force it not only to yield, but so to rave that it in one breath calls life happy and recommends it to be given up? For who is so blind as not to see that if it were happy it would not be fled from? And if they say we should flee from it on account of the infirmities that beset it, why then do they not lower their pride and acknowledge that it is miserable? Was it, I would ask, fortitude or weakness which prompted Cato to kill himself? for he would not have done so had he not been too weak to endure Cæsar's victory. Where, then, is his fortitude? It has yielded, it has succumbed, it has been so thoroughly overcome as to abandon, forsake, flee this happy life. Or was it no longer happy? Then it was miserable. How, then, were these not evils which made life miserable, and a thing to be escaped from?

And therefore those who admit that these are evils, as the Peripatetics do, and the Old Academy, the sect which Varro advocates, express a more intelligible doctrine; but theirs also is a surprising mistake, for they contend that this is a happy life which is beset by these evils, even though they be so great that he who endures them should commit suicide to escape them. "Pains and anguish of body," says Varro, "are evils, and so much the worse in proportion to their severity; and to escape them you must quit this life." What life, I pray? This life, he says, which is oppressed by such evils. Then it is happy in the midst of these very evils on account of which you say we must quit it? Or do you call it happy because you are at liberty to escape these evils by death? What, then, if by some secret judgment of God you were held fast and not permitted to die, nor suffered to live without these evils? In that case, at least, you would say that such a life was miserable. It is soon relinquished, no doubt, but this does not make it not miserable; for were it eternal, you yourself would pronounce it miserable. Its brevity, therefore, does not clear it of misery; neither ought it to be called happiness because it is a brief misery. Certainly there is a mighty force in these evils which compel a man——according to them, even a wise man——to cease to be a man that he may escape them, though they say, and say truly, that it is as it were the first and strongest demand of nature that a man cherish himself, and naturally therefore avoid death, and should so stand his own friend as to wish and vehemently aim at continuing to exist as a living creature, and subsisting in this union of soul and body. There is a mighty force in these evils to overcome this natural instinct by which death is by every means

and with all a man's efforts avoided, and to overcome it
so completely that what was avoided is desired, sought
after, and if it cannot in any other way be obtained, is
inflicted by the man on himself. There is a mighty
force in these evils which make fortitude a homicide—
if, indeed, that is to be called fortitude which is so
thoroughly overcome by these evils, that it not only
cannot preserve by patience the man whom it undertook to govern and defend, but is itself obliged to kill
him. The wise man, I admit, ought to bear death with
patience, but when it is inflicted by another. If, then, as
these men maintain, he is obliged to inflict it on himself, certainly it must be owned that the ills which compel him to this are not only evils, but intolerable evils.
The life, then, which is either subject to accidents, or
environed with evils so considerable and grievous, could
never have been called happy, if the men who give it this
name had condescended to yield to the truth, and to be
conquered by valid arguments, when they inquired
after the happy life, as they yield to unhappiness, and
are overcome by overwhelming evils, when they put
themselves to death, and if they had not fancied that
the supreme good was to be found in this mortal life;
for the very virtues of this life, which are certainly its
best and most useful possessions, are all the more telling proofs of its miseries in proportion as they are helpful against the violence of its dangers, toils, and woes.

For if these are true virtues—and such cannot exist save in those who have true piety—they do not profess to be able to deliver the men who possess them from all miseries; for true virtues tell no such lies, but they profess that by the hope of the future world this life, which is miserably involved in the many and great evils of this world, is happy as it is also safe. For if not yet safe, how could it be happy? And therefore the Apostle Paul, speaking not of men without prudence, temperance, fortitude, and justice, but of those whose lives were regulated by true piety, and whose virtues were therefore true, says, "For we are saved by hope: now hope which is seen is not hope; for what a man seeth, why doth he yet hope for? But if we hope for that we see not, then do we with patience wait for it." As, therefore, we are saved, so we are made happy by hope. And as we do not as yet possess a present, but look for a future salvation, so is it with our happiness, and this "with patience"; for we are encompassed with evils, which we ought patiently to endure, until we come to the ineffable enjoyment of unmixed good; for there shall be no longer anything to endure. Salvation, such as it shall be in the world to come, shall itself be our final happiness. And this happiness these philosophers refuse to believe in, because they do not see it, and attempt to fabricate for themselves a happiness in this life, based upon a virtue which is as deceitful as it is proud.

CHAPTER 5

OF THE SOCIAL LIFE, WHICH, THOUGH MOST DESIRABLE,

IS FREQUENTLY DISTURBED BY MANY DISTRESSES

We give a much more unlimited approval to their idea that the life of the wise man must be social. For how could the city of God (concerning which we are already writing no less than the nineteenth book of this work) either take a beginning or be developed, or attain its proper destiny, if the life of the saints were not a social life? But who can enumerate all the great grievances with which human society abounds in the misery of this mortal state? Who can weigh them? Hear how one of their comic writers makes one of his characters express the common feelings of all men in this matter: "I am married; this is one misery. Children are born to me; they are additional cares." What shall I say of the miseries of love which Terence also recounts—"slights, suspicions, quarrels, war to-day, peace to-morrow?" Is not human life full of such things? Do they not often occur even in honorable friendships? On all hands we experience these slights, suspicions, quarrels, war, all of which are undoubted evils; while, on the other hand, peace is a doubtful good, because we do not know the heart of our friend, and though we did know it to-day, we should be as ignorant of what it might be to-morrow. Who ought to be, or who are more friendly than those who live in the same family? And yet who can rely even upon this friendship, seeing that secret treachery has often broken it up, and produced enmity as bitter as the amity was sweet, or seemed sweet by the most perfect dissimulation? It is on this account that the words of Cicero so move the heart of every one, and provoke a sigh: "There are no snares more dangerous than those which lurk under the guise of duty or the name of relationship. For the man who is your declared foe you can easily baffle by precaution; but this hidden, intestine, and domestic danger not merely exists, but overwhelms you before you can foresee and examine it." It is also to this that allusion is made by the divine saying, "A man's foes are those of his own household"—words which one cannot hear without pain; for though a man have sufficient fortitude to endure it with equanimity, and sufficient sagacity to baffle the malice of a pretended friend, yet if he himself is a good man, he cannot but be greatly pained at the discovery of the perfidy of wicked men, whether they have always been wicked and merely feigned goodness, or have fallen from a better to a malicious disposition. If, then, home, the natural refuge from the ills of life, is itself not safe, what shall we say of the city, which, as it is larger, is so much the more filled with lawsuits civil and criminal, and is never free from the fear, if sometimes from the actual outbreak, of disturbing and bloody insurrections and civil wars?

In the following chapter Augustine digresses to articulate his view of earthly punishment and his hostility to torture as a means of investigating the truth.

CHAPTER 6

OF THE ERROR OF HUMAN JUDGMENTS

WHEN THE TRUTH IS HIDDEN

What shall I say of these judgments which men pronounce on men, and which are necessary in communities, whatever outward peace they enjoy? Melancholy and lamentable judgments they are, since the judges are men who cannot discern the consciences of those at their bar, and are therefore frequently compelled to put innocent witnesses to the torture to ascertain the truth regarding the crimes of other men. What shall I say of torture applied to the accused himself? He is tortured to discover whether he is guilty, so that, though innocent, he suffers most undoubted punishment for crime that is still doubtful, not because it is proved that he committed it, but because it is not ascertained that he did not commit it. Thus the ignorance of the judge frequently involves an innocent person in suffering. And what is still more unendurable—a thing, indeed, to be bewailed, and, if that were possible, watered with fountains of tears—is this, that when the judge puts the accused to the question, that he may not unwittingly put an innocent man to death, the result of this lamentable ignorance is that this very person, whom he tortured that he might not condemn him if innocent, is condemned to death both tortured and innocent. For if he has chosen, in obedience to the philosophical instructions to the wise man, to quit this life rather than endure any longer such tortures, he declares that he has committed the crime which in fact he has not committed. And when he has been condemned and put to death, the judge is still in ignorance whether he has put to death an innocent or a guilty person, though he put the accused to the torture for the very purpose of saving himself from condemning the innocent; and consequently he has both tortured an innocent man to discover his innocence, and has put him to death without discovering it. If such darkness shrouds social life, will a wise judge take his seat on the bench or no? Beyond question he will. For human society, which he thinks it a wickedness to abandon, constrains him and compels him to this duty. And he thinks it no wickedness that innocent witnesses are tortured regarding the crimes of which other men are accused; or that the accused are put to the torture, so that they are often overcome with anguish, and, though innocent, make false confessions regarding themselves, and are punished; or that, though they be not condemned to die, they often die during, or in consequence of, the torture; or that sometimes the accusers, who perhaps have been prompted by a desire to benefit society by bringing criminals to justice, are themselves condemned through the ignorance of the judge, because they are unable to prove the truth of their accusations though they are true, and because the witnesses lie, and the accused endures the torture without being moved to confession. These numerous and important evils he does not consider sins; for the wise judge does these things, not with any intention of doing harm, but because his ignorance compels him, and because human society claims him as a judge. But though we therefore acquit the judge of malice, we must none the less condemn human life as miserable. And if he is compelled to torture and punish the innocent because his office and his ignorance constrain him, is he a happy as well as a guiltless man? Surely it were proof of more profound considerateness and finer feeling were he to recognize the misery of these necessities, and shrink from his own implication in that misery; and had he any piety about him, he would cry to God "From my necessities deliver Thou me."

The subject of war follows naturally from that of punishment.

CHAPTER 7

OF THE DIVERSITY OF LANGUAGES, BY WHICH THE

INTERCOURSE OF MEN IS PREVENTED; AND OF THE

MISERY OF WARS, EVEN OF THOSE CALLED JUST

After the state or city comes the world, the third circle of human society—the first being the house, and the second the city. And the world, as it is larger, so it is fuller of dangers, as the greater sea is the more dangerous. And here, in the first place, man is separated from man by the difference of languages. For if two men, each ignorant of the other's language, meet, and are not compelled to pass, but, on the contrary, to remain in company, dumb animals, though of different species, would more easily hold intercourse than they, human beings though they be. For their common nature is no help to friendliness when they are prevented by diversity of language from conveying their sentiments to one another; so that a man would more readily hold intercourse with his dog than with a foreigner. But the imperial city has endeavored to impose on subject nations not only her yoke, but her language, as a bond of peace, so that interpreters, far from being scarce, are numberless. This is true; but how many great wars, how much slaughter and bloodshed, have provided this unity! And though these are past, the end of these miseries has not yet come. For though there have never been wanting, nor are yet wanting, hostile nations beyond the empire, against whom wars have been and are waged, yet, supposing there were no such nations, the very extent of the empire itself has produced wars of a more obnoxious description—social and civil wars—and with these the whole race has been agitated, either by the actual conflict or the fear of a renewed outbreak. If I attempted to give an adequate description of these manifold disasters, these stern and lasting necessities, though I am quite unequal to the task, what limit could I set? But, say they, the wise man will wage just wars. As if he would not all the rather lament the necessity of just wars, if he remembers that he is a man; for if they were not just he would not wage them, and would therefore be delivered from all wars. For it is the wrongdoing of the opposing party which compels the wise man to wage just wars; and this wrong-doing, even though it gave rise to no war, would still be matter of grief to man because it is man's wrong-doing. Let every one, then, who thinks with pain on all these great evils, so horrible, so ruthless, acknowledge that this is misery. And if any one either endures or thinks of them without mental pain, this is a more miserable plight still, for he thinks himself happy because he has lost human feeling.

CHAPTER 8

THAT THE FRIENDSHIP OF GOOD MEN CANNOT
BE SECURELY RESTED IN, SO LONG AS THE DANGERS
OF THIS LIFE FORCE US TO BE ANXIOUS

In our present wretched condition we frequently mistake a friend for an enemy, and an enemy for a friend. And if we escape this pitiable blindness, is not the unfeigned confidence and mutual love of true and good friends our one solace in human society, filled as it is with misunderstandings and calamities? And yet the more friends we have, and the more widely they are scattered, the more numerous are our fears that some portion of the vast masses of the disasters of life may light upon them. For we are not only anxious lest they suffer from famine, war, disease, captivity, or the inconceivable horrors of slavery, but we are also affected with the much more painful dread that their friendship may be changed into perfidy, malice, and injustice. And when these contingencies actually occur—as they do the more frequently the more friends we have, and the more widely they are scattered—and when they come to our knowledge, who but the man who has experienced it can tell with what pangs the heart is torn? We would, in fact, prefer to hear that they were dead, although we could not without anguish hear of even this. For if their life has solaced us with the charms of friendship, can it be that their death should affect us with no sadness? He who will have none of this sadness must, if possible, have no friendly intercourse. Let him interdict or extinguish friendly affection; let him burst with ruthless insensibility the bonds of every human relationship; or let him contrive so to use them that no sweetness shall distil into his spirit. But if this is utterly impossible, how shall we contrive to feel no bitterness in the death of those whose life has been sweet to us? Hence arises that grief which affects the tender heart like a wound or a bruise, and which is healed by the application of kindly consolation. For though the cure is affected all the more easily and rapidly the better condition the soul is in, we must not on this account suppose that there is nothing at all to heal. Although, then, our present life is afflicted, sometimes in a milder, sometimes in a more painful degree, by the death of those very dear to us, and especially of useful public men, yet we would prefer to hear that such men were dead rather than to hear or perceive that they had fallen from the faith, or from virtue—in other words, that they were spiritually dead. Of this vast material for misery the earth is full, and therefore it is written, "Is not human life upon earth a trial?" And with the same reference the Lord says. "Woe to the world because of offenses!" and again, "Because iniquity abounded, the love of many shall wax cold." And hence we enjoy some gratification when our good friends die;

for though their death leaves us in sorrow, we have the consolatory assurance that they are beyond the ills by which in this life even the best of men are broken down or corrupted, or are in danger of both results.

CHAPTER 10

THE REWARD PREPARED FOR THE SAINTS AFTER
THEY HAVE ENDURED THE TRIAL OF THIS LIFE

But not even the saints and faithful worshippers of the one true and most high God are safe from the manifold temptations and deceits of the demons. For in this abode of weakness, and in these wicked days, this state of anxiety has also its use, stimulating us to seek with keener longing for that security where peace is complete and unassailable. There we shall enjoy the gifts of nature, that is to say, all that God the Creator of all natures has bestowed upon ours—gifts not only good, but eternal—not only of the spirit, healed now by wisdom, but also of the body renewed by the resurrection. There the virtues shall no longer be struggling against any vice or evil, but shall enjoy the reward of victory, the eternal peace which no adversary shall disturb. This is the final blessedness, this the ultimate consummation, the unending end. Here, indeed, we are said to be blessed when we have such peace as can be enjoyed in a good life; but such blessedness is mere misery compared to that final felicity. When we mortals possess such peace as this mortal life can afford, virtue, if we are living rightly, makes a right use of the advantages of this peaceful condition; and when we have it not, virtue makes a good use even of the evils a man suffers. But this is true virtue, when it refers all the advantages it makes a good use of, and all that it does in making good use of good and evil things, and itself also, to that end in which we shall enjoy the best and greatest peace possible.

CHAPTER II

OF THE HAPPINESS OF THE ETERNAL PEACE,

WHICH CONSTITUTES THE END OR

TRUE PERFECTION OF THE SAINTS

And thus we may say of peace, as we have said of eternal life, that it is the end of our good; and the rather because the Psalmist says of the city of God, the subject of this laborious work, "Praise the Lord, O Jerusalem; praise thy God, O Zion: for He hath strengthened the bars of thy gates; He hath blessed thy children within thee; who hath made thy borders peace." For when the bars of her gates shall be strengthened, none shall go in or come out from her; consequently we ought to understand the peace of her borders as that final peace we are wishing to declare. For even the mystical name of the city itself, that is, Jerusalem, means, as I have already said, "Vision of Peace." But as the

word peace is employed in connection with things in
this world in which certainly life eternal has no place,
we have preferred to call the end or supreme good of
this city life eternal rather than peace. Of this end the
apostle says, "But now, being freed from sin, and
become servants to God, ye have your fruit unto holi-
ness, and the end life eternal." But, on the other hand,
as those who are not familiar with Scripture may suppose that the life of the wicked is eternal life, either
because of the immortality of the soul, which some of
the philosophers even have recognized, or because of
the endless punishment of the wicked, which forms a
part of our faith, and which seems impossible unless
the wicked live for ever, it may therefore be advisable,
in order that every one may readily understand what
we mean, to say that the end or supreme good of this
city is either peace in eternal life, or eternal life in
peace. For peace is a good so great, that even in this
earthly and mortal life there is no word we hear with
such pleasure, nothing we desire with such zest, or find
to be more thoroughly gratifying. So that if we dwell
for a little longer on this subject, we shall not, in my
opinion, be wearisome to our readers, who will attend
both for the sake of understanding what is the end of
this city of which we speak, and for the sake of the
sweetness of peace which is dear to all.

CHAPTER 12

THAT EVEN THE FIERCENESS OF WAR AND ALL THE DISQUIETUDE OF MEN MAKE TOWARDS THIS ONE END OF PEACE, WHICH EVERY NATURE DESIRES

Whoever gives even moderate attention to human affairs and to our common nature, will recognize that if there is no man who does not wish to be joyful, neither is there any one who does not wish to have peace. For even they who make war desire nothing but victory—desire, that is to say, to attain to peace with glory. For what else is victory than the conquest of those who resist us? and when this is done there is peace. It is therefore with the desire for peace that wars are waged, even by those who take pleasure in exercising their warlike nature in command and battle. And hence it is obvious that peace is the end sought for by war. For every man seeks peace by waging war, but no man seeks war by making peace. For even they who intentionally interrupt the peace in which they are living have no hatred of peace, but only wish it changed into a peace that suits them better. They do not, therefore, wish to have no peace, but only one more to their mind. And in the case of sedition, when men have separated themselves from the community, they yet do not effect what they wish, unless they maintain some kind of peace with their fellow-conspirators. And therefore even robbers take care to maintain peace with their comrades, that they may with greater effect and greater safety invade the peace of other men. And if an individual happen to be of such unrivalled strength, and to be so jealous of partnership, that he trusts himself with no comrades, but makes his own plots, and commits depredations and murders on his own account, yet he maintains some shadow of peace with such persons as he is unable to kill, and from whom he wishes to conceal his deeds. In his own home, too, he makes it his aim to be at peace with his wife and children, and any other members of his household; for unquestionably their prompt obedience to his every look is a source of pleasure to him. And if this be not rendered, he is angry, he chides and punishes; and even by this storm he secures the calm peace of his own home, as occasion demands. For he sees that peace cannot be maintained unless all the members of the same domestic circle be subject to one head, such as he himself is in his own house. And therefore if a city or nation offered to submit itself to him, to serve him in the same style as he had made his household serve him, he would no longer lurk in a brigand's hiding-places, but lift his head in open day as a king, though the same coveteousness and wickedness should remain in him. And thus all men desire to have peace with their own circle whom they wish to govern as suits themselves. For even those whom they make war against they wish to make their own, and impose on them the laws of their own peace.

But let us suppose a man such as poetry and mythology speak of—a man so insociable and savage as to be called rather a semi-man than a man. Although, then, his kingdom was the solitude of a dreary cave, and he himself was so singularly bad-hearted that he was named Κακός, which is the Greek word for bad; though he had no wife to soothe him with endearing talk, no children to play with, no sons to do his bidding, no friend to enliven him with intercourse, not even his father Vulcan (though in one respect he was happier than his father, not having begotten a monster like himself); although he gave to no man, but took as he wished whatever he could, from whomsoever he could, when he could; yet in that solitary den, the floor of which, as Virgil says, was always reeking with recent slaughter, there was nothing else than peace sought, a peace in which no one should molest him, or disquiet him with any assault or alarm. With his own body he desired to be at peace, and he was satisfied only in proportion as he had this peace. For he ruled his members, and they obeyed him; and for the sake of pacifying his mortal nature, which rebelled when it needed anything, and of allaying the sedition of hunger which threatened to banish the soul from the body, he made forays, slew, and devoured, but used the ferocity and savageness he displayed in these actions only for the preservation of his own life's peace. So that, had he been willing to make with other men the same peace which he made with himself in his own cave, he would neither have been called bad, nor a monster, nor a semi-man. Or if the appearance of his body and his vomiting smoky fires frightened men from having any dealings with him, perhaps his fierce ways arose not from a desire to do mischief, but from the necessity of finding a living. But he may have had no existence, or, at least, he was not such as the poets fancifully describe him, for they had to exalt Hercules, and did so at the expense of Cacus. It is better, then, to believe that such a man or semi-man never existed, and that this, in common with many other fancies of the poets, is mere fiction. For the most savage animals (and he is said to have been almost a wild beast) encompass their own species with a ring of protecting peace. They cohabit, beget, produce, suckle, and bring up their young, though very many of them are not gregarious, but solitary—not like sheep, deer, pigeons, starlings, bees, but such as lions, foxes, eagles, bats. For what tigress does not gently purr over her cubs, and lay aside her ferocity to fondle them? What kite, solitary as he is when circling over his prey, does not seek a mate, build a nest, hatch the eggs, bring up the young birds, and maintain with the mother of his family as peaceful a domestic alliance as he can? How much more powerfully do the laws of man's nature move him to hold fellowship and maintain peace with all men so far as in him lies, since even wicked men wage war to maintain the peace of their own circle, and wish that, if possible, all men belonged to them, that all men and things might serve but one head, and might, either through love or fear, yield themselves to peace with him! It is thus that pride in its perversity apes God. It abhors equality with other men under Him; but, instead of His rule, it seeks to impose a rule of its own upon its equals. It abhors, that is to say, the just peace of God, and loves its own unjust peace; but it cannot help loving peace of one kind or other. For there is no vice so clean contrary to nature that it obliterates even the faintest traces of nature.

He, then, who prefers what is right to what is wrong, and what is well-ordered to what is perverted, sees that the peace of unjust men is not worthy to be called peace in comparison with the peace of the just. And yet even what is perverted must of necessity be in harmony with, and in dependence on, and in some part of the order of things, for otherwise it would have no existence at all. Suppose a man hangs with his head downwards, this is certainly a perverted attitude of body and arrangement of its members; for that which nature requires to be above is beneath, and vice versâ. This perversity disturbs the peace of the body, and is therefore painful. Nevertheless the spirit is at peace with its body, and labors for its preservation, and hence the suffering; but if it is banished from the body by its pains, then, so long as the bodily framework holds together, there is in the remains a kind of peace among the members, and hence the body remains suspended. And inasmuch as the earthly body tends towards the earth, and rests on the bond by which it is suspended, it tends thus to its natural peace, and the voice of its own weight demands a place for it to rest; and though now lifeless and without feeling, it does not fall from the peace that is natural to its place in creation, whether it already has it, or is tending towards it. For if you apply embalming preparations to prevent the bodily frame from mouldering and dissolving, a kind of peace still unites part to part, and keeps the whole body in a suitable place on the earth—in other words, in a place that is at peace with the body. If, on the other hand, the body receive no such care, but be left to the natural course, it is disturbed by exhalations that do not harmonize with one another, and that offend our senses; for it is this which is perceived in putrefaction until it is assimilated to the elements of the world, and particle by particle enters into peace with them. Yet throughout this process the laws of the most high Creator and Governor are strictly observed, for it is by Him the peace of the universe is administered. For although minute animals are produced from the carcass of a larger animal, all these little atoms, by the law of the same Creator, serve the animals they belong to in peace. And although the flesh of dead animals be eaten by others, no matter where it be carried, nor what it be brought into contact with, nor what it be converted and changed into, it still is ruled by the same laws which pervade all things for the conservation of every mortal race, and which bring things that fit one another into harmony.

CHAPTER 13

OF THE UNIVERSAL PEACE WHICH THE LAW OF NATURE
PRESERVES THROUGH ALL DISTURBANCES,
AND BY WHICH EVERY ONE REACHES HIS DESERT
IN A WAY REGULATED BY THE JUST JUDGE

The peace of the body then consists in the duly proportioned arrangement of its parts. The peace of the irrational soul is the harmonious repose of the appetites, and that of the rational soul the harmony of knowledge and action. The peace of body and soul is the well-ordered and harmonious life and health of the living creature. Peace between man and God is the well-ordered obedience of faith to eternal law. Peace between man and man is well-ordered concord. Domestic peace is the well-ordered concord between those of the family who rule and those who obey. Civil peace is a similar concord among the citizens. The peace of the celestial city is the perfectly ordered and harmonious enjoyment

of God, and of one another in God. The peace of all
things is the tranquillity of order. Order is the distribu-
tion which allots things equal and unequal, each to its
own place. And hence, though the miserable, in so far as
they are such, do certainly not enjoy peace, but are sev-
ered from that tranquillity of order in which there is no
disturbance, nevertheless, inasmuch as they are deservedly and justly miserable, they are by their very misery
connected with order. They are not, indeed, conjoined
with the blessed, but they are disjoined from them by
the law of order. And though they are disquieted, their
circumstances are notwithstanding adjusted to them,
and consequently they have some tranquillity of order,
and therefore some peace. But they are wretched because,
although not wholly miserable, they are not in that
place where any mixture of misery is impossible. They
would, however, be more wretched if they had not that
peace which arises from being in harmony with the
natural order of things. When they suffer, their peace is
in so far disturbed; but their peace continues in so far
as they do not suffer, and in so far as their nature continues to exist. As, then, there may be life without pain,
while there cannot be pain without some kind of life, so
there may be peace without war, but there cannot be
war without some kind of peace, because war supposes
the existence of some natures to wage it, and these
natures cannot exist without peace of one kind or other.

And therefore there is a nature in which evil does not or even cannot exist; but there cannot be a nature in which there is no good. Hence not even the nature of the devil himself is evil, in so far as it is nature, but it was made evil by being perverted. Thus he did not abide in the truth, but could not escape the judgment of the Truth; he did not abide in the tranquillity of order, but did not therefore escape the power of the Ordainer. The good imparted by God to his nature did not screen him from the justice of God by which order was preserved in his punishment; neither did God punish the good which He had created, but the evil which the devil had committed. God did not take back all He had imparted to his nature, but something He took and something He left, that there might remain enough to be sensible of the loss of what was taken. And this very sensibility to pain is evidence of the good which has been taken away and the good which has been left. For, were nothing good left, there could be no pain on account of the good which had been lost. For he who sins is still worse if he rejoices in his loss of righteousness. But he who is in pain, if he derives no benefit from it, mourns at least the loss of health. And as righteousness and health are both good things, and as the loss of any good thing is matter of grief, not of joy—if, at least, there is no compensation, as spiritual righteousness may compensate for the loss of bodily health—certainly it is more suit-

able for a wicked man to grieve in punishment than to
rejoice in his fault. As, then, the joy of a sinner who has
abandoned what is good is evidence of a bad will, so his
grief for the good he has lost when he is punished is
evidence of a good nature. For he who laments the peace
his nature has lost is stirred to do so by some relics of
peace which make his nature friendly to itself. And it is
very just that in the final punishment the wicked and
godless should in anguish bewail the loss of the natural
advantages they enjoyed, and should perceive that they
were most justly taken from them by that God whose
benign liberality they had despised. God, then, the most
wise Creator and most just Ordainer of all natures, who
placed the human race upon earth as its greatest orna-
ment, imparted to men some good things adapted to
this life, to wit, temporal peace, such as we can enjoy in
this life from health and safety and human fellowship,
and all things needful for the preservation and recovery
of this peace, such as the objects which are accommo-
dated to our outward senses, light, night, the air, and
waters suitable for us, and everything the body requires
to sustain, shelter, heal, or beautify it: and all under this
most equitable condition, that every man who made a
good use of these advantages suited to the peace of this
mortal condition, should receive ampler and better
blessings, namely, the peace of immortality, accompanied by glory and honor in an endless life made fit for

the enjoyment of God and of one another in God; but that he who used the present blessings badly should both lose them and should not receive the others.

CHAPTER 14

OF THE ORDER AND LAW WHICH OBTAIN IN HEAVEN
AND EARTH, WHEREBY IT COMES TO PASS THAT HUMAN
SOCIETY IS SERVED BY THOSE WHO RULE IT

The whole use, then, of things temporal has a reference to this result of earthly peace in the earthly community, while in the city of God it is connected with eternal peace. And therefore, if we were irrational animals, we should desire nothing beyond the proper arrangement of the parts of the body and the satisfaction of the appetites—nothing, therefore, but bodily comfort and abundance of pleasures, that the peace of the body might contribute to the peace of the soul. For if bodily peace be awanting, a bar is put to the peace even of the irrational soul, since it cannot obtain the gratification of its appetites. And these two together help out the mutual peace of soul and body, the peace of harmonious life and health. For as animals, by shunning pain, show that they love bodily peace, and, by pursuing pleasure to gratify their appetites, show that they love peace of soul, so their shrinking from death is a sufficient indication of their intense love of that peace which binds soul and body in close alliance. But, as man has a rational soul, he subordinates all this which he has in common with the beasts to the peace of his rational soul, that his intellect may have free play and may regulate his actions, and that he may thus enjoy the well-ordered harmony of knowledge and action which constitutes, as we have said, the peace of the rational soul. And for this purpose he must desire to be neither molested by pain, nor disturbed by desire, nor extinguished by death, that he may arrive at some useful knowledge by which he may regulate his life and manners. But, owing to the liability of the human mind to fall into mistakes, this very pursuit of knowledge may be a snare to him unless he has a divine Master, whom he may obey without misgiving, and who may at the same time give him such help as to preserve his own freedom. And because, so long as he is in this mortal body, he is a stranger to God, he walks by faith, not by sight; and he therefore refers all peace, bodily or spiritual or both, to that peace which mortal man has with the immortal God, so that he exhibits the well-ordered obedience of faith to eternal law. But as this divine Master inculcates two precepts—the love of God and the love of our neighbor—and as in these precepts a man finds three things he has to love—God, himself, and his neighbor—and that he who loves God loves himself thereby, it follows that he must endeavor to get his neighbor to love God, since he is ordered to love his neighbor as himself. He ought to make this endeavor in behalf of his wife, his children, his household, all within his reach, even as he would wish his neighbor to do the same for him if he needed it; and consequently he will be at peace, or in well-ordered concord, with all men, as far as in him lies. And this is the order of this concord, that a man, in the first place, injure no one, and, in the second, do good to every one he can reach. Primarily, therefore, his own household are his care, for the law of nature and of society gives him readier access to them and greater opportunity of serving them. And hence the apostle says, "Now, if any provide not for his own, and specially for those of his own house, he hath denied the faith, and is worse than an infidel." This is the origin of domestic peace, or the well-ordered concord of those in the family who rule and those who obey. For they who care for the rest rule—the husband the wife, the parents the children, the masters the servants; and they who are cared for obey—the women their husbands, the children their parents, the servants their masters. But in the family of the just man who lives by faith and is as yet a pilgrim journeying on to the celestial city, even those who rule serve those whom they seem to command; for they rule not from a love of power, but from a sense of the duty they owe to others—not because they are proud of authority, but because they love mercy.

CHAPTER 15

OF THE LIBERTY PROPER TO MAN'S NATURE, AND THE

SERVITUDE INTRODUCED BY SIN—A SERVITUDE IN

WHICH THE MAN WHOSE WILL IS WICKED IS THE

SLAVE OF HIS OWN LUST, THOUGH HE IS FREE

SO FAR AS REGARDS OTHER MEN

This is prescribed by the order of nature: it is thus that God has created man. For "let them," He says, "have dominion over the fish of the sea, and over the fowl of the air, and over every creeping thing which creepeth on the earth." He did not intend that His rational creature, who was made in His image, should have dominion over anything but the irrational creation—not man over man, but man over the beasts. And hence the righteous men in primitive times were made shepherds of cattle rather than kings of men, God intending thus to teach us what the relative position of the creatures is, and what the desert of sin; for it is with justice, we believe, that the condition of slavery is the result of sin. And this is why we do not find the word "slave" in any part of Scripture until righteous Noah branded the sin of his son with this name. It is a name, therefore, introduced by sin and not by nature. The origin of the Latin word for slave is supposed to be found in the circumstance that those who by the law of war were liable to be killed were sometimes preserved by their victors, and were hence called servants. And these circumstances could never have arisen save through sin. For even when we wage a just war, our adversaries must be sinning; and every victory, even though gained by wicked men, is a result of the first judgment of God, who humbles the vanquished either for the sake of removing or of punishing their sins. Witness that man of God, Daniel, who, when he was in captivity, confessed to God his own sins and the sins of his people, and declares with pious grief that these were the cause of the captivity. The prime cause, then, of slavery is sin, which brings man under the dominion of his fellow—that which does not happen save by the judgment of God, with whom is no unrighteousness, and who knows how to award fit punishments to every variety of offence. But our Master in heaven says, "Every one who doeth sin is the servant of sin." And thus there are many wicked masters who have religious men as their slaves, and who are yet themselves in bondage; "for of whom a man is overcome, of the same is he brought in bondage." And beyond question it is a happier thing to be the slave of a man than of a lust; for even this very lust of ruling, to mention no others, lays waste men's hearts with the most ruthless dominion. Moreover, when men are subjected to one another in a peaceful order, the lowly position does as much good to the servant as the proud position does harm to the master. But by nature, as God first created us, no one is the slave either of man or of sin. This servitude is, however, penal, and is appointed by that law which enjoins the preservation of the natural order and forbids its disturbance; for if nothing had been done in violation of that law, there would have been nothing to restrain by penal servitude. And therefore the apostle admonishes slaves to be subject to their masters, and to serve them heartily and with good-will, so that, if they cannot be freed by their masters, they may themselves make their slavery in some sort free, by serving not in crafty fear, but in faithful love, until all unrighteousness pass away, and all principality and every human power be brought to nothing, and God be all in all.

CHAPTER 16

OF EQUITABLE RULE

And therefore, although our righteous fathers had slaves, and administered their domestic affairs so as to distinguish between the condition of slaves and the heirship of sons in regard to the blessings of this life, yet in regard to the worship of God, in whom we hope for eternal blessings, they took an equally loving oversight of all the members of their household. And this is so much in accordance with the natural order, that the head of the household was called paterfamilias; and this name has been so generally accepted, that even those whose rule is unrighteous are glad to apply it to themselves. But those who are true fathers of their households desire and endeavor that all the members of their household, equally with their own children, should worship and win God, and should come to that heavenly home in which the duty of ruling men is no longer necessary, because the duty of caring for their everlasting happiness has also ceased; but, until they reach that home, masters ought to feel their position of authority a greater burden than servants their service. And if any member of the family interrupts the domestic peace by disobedience, he is corrected either by word or blow, or some kind of just and legitimate punishment, such as society permits, that he may himself be the better for it, and be readjusted to the family harmony from which he had dislocated himself. For as it is not benevolent to give a man help at the expense of some greater benefit he might receive, so it is not innocent to spare a man at the risk of his falling into graver sin. To be innocent, we must not only do harm to no man, but also restrain him from sin or punish his sin, so that either the man himself who is punished may profit by his experience, or others be warned by his example. Since, then, the house ought to be the beginning or element of the city, and every beginning bears reference to some end of its own kind, and every element to the integrity of the whole of which it is an element, it follows plainly enough that domestic peace has a relation to civic peace—in other words, that the well-ordered concord of domestic obedience and domestic rule has a relation to the well-ordered concord of civic obedience and civic rule. And therefore it follows, further, that the father of the family ought to frame his domestic rule in accordance with the law of the city, so that the household may be in harmony with the civic order.

CHAPTER 17

WHAT PRODUCES PEACE, AND WHAT DISCORD,
BETWEEN THE HEAVENLY AND EARTHLY CITIES

But the families which do not live by faith seek their peace in the earthly advantages of this life; while the families which live by faith look for those eternal blessings which are promised, and use as pilgrims such advantages of time and of earth as do not fascinate and divert them from God, but rather aid them to endure with greater ease, and to keep down the number of those burdens of the corruptible body which weigh upon the soul. Thus the things necessary for this mortal life are used by both kinds of men and families alike, but each has its own peculiar and widely different aim in using them. The earthly city, which does not live by faith, seeks an earthly peace, and the end it proposes, in the well-ordered concord of civic obedience and rule, is the combination of men's wills to attain the things which are helpful to this life. The heavenly city, or rather the part of it which sojourns on earth and lives by faith, makes use of this peace only because it must, until this mortal condition which necessitates it shall pass away. Consequently, so long as it lives like a captive and a stranger in the earthly city, though it has already received the promise of redemption, and the gift of the Spirit as the earnest of it, it makes no scruple to obey the laws of the earthly city, whereby the things necessary for the maintenance of this mortal life are administered; and thus, as this life is common to both cities, so there is a harmony between them in regard to what belongs to it. But, as the earthly city has had some philosophers whose doctrine is condemned by the divine teaching, and who, being deceived either by their own conjectures or by demons, supposed that many gods must be invited to take an interest in human affairs, and assigned to each a separate function and a separate department—to one the body, to another the soul; and in the body itself, to one the head, to another the neck, and each of the other members to one of the gods; and in like manner, in the soul, to one god the natural capacity was assigned, to another education, to another anger, to another lust; and so the various affairs of life were assigned—cattle to one, corn to another, wine to another, oil to another, the woods to another, money to another, navigation to another, wars and victories to another, marriages to another, births and fecundity to another, and other things to other gods: and as the celestial city, on the other hand, knew that one God only was to be worshipped, and that to Him alone was due that service which the Greeks call λατρεία, and which can be given only to a god, it has come to pass that the two cities could not have common laws of religion, and that the heavenly city has been compelled in this matter to dissent, and to become obnoxious to those who think differently, and to stand the brunt of their anger and hatred and persecutions, except in so far as the minds of their enemies have been alarmed by the multitude of the Christians and quelled by the manifest protection of God accorded to them. This heavenly city, then, while it sojourns on earth, calls citizens out of all nations, and gathers together a society of pilgrims of all languages, not scrupling about diversities in the manners, laws, and institutions whereby earthly peace is secured and maintained, but recognizing that, however various these are, they all tend to one and the same end of earthly peace. It therefore is so far from rescinding and abolishing these diversities, that it even preserves and adopts them, so long only as no hindrance to the worship of the one supreme and true God is thus introduced. Even the heavenly city, therefore, while in its state of pilgrimage, avails itself of the peace of earth, and, so far as it can without injuring faith and godliness, desires and maintains a common agreement among men regarding the acquisition of the necessaries of life, and makes this earthly peace bear upon the peace of heaven; for this alone can be truly called and esteemed the peace of the reasonable creatures, consisting as it does in the perfectly ordered and harmonious enjoyment of God and of one another in God. When we shall have reached that peace, this mortal life shall give place to one that is eternal, and our body shall be no more this animal body which by its corruption weighs down the soul, but a spiritual body feeling no want, and in all its members subjected to the will. In its pilgrim state the heavenly city possesses this peace by faith; and by this faith it lives righteously when it refers to the attainment of that peace every good action towards God and man; for the life of the city is a social life.

CHAPTER 18

HOW DIFFERENT THE UNCERTAINTY OF THE NEW ACADEMY IS FROM THE CERTAINTY OF THE CHRISTIAN FAITH

As regards the uncertainty about everything which Varro alleges to be the differentiating characteristic of the New Academy, the city of God thoroughly detests such doubt as madness. Regarding matters which it apprehends by the mind and reason it has most absolute certainty, although its knowledge is limited because of the corruptible body pressing down the mind, for, as the apostle says, "We know in part." It believes also the evidence of the senses which the mind uses by aid of the body; for [if one who trusts his senses is sometimes deceived], he is more wretchedly deceived who fancies he should never trust them. It believes also the Holy Scriptures, old and new, which we call canonical, and which are the source of the faith by which the just lives and by which we walk without doubting whilst we are absent from the Lord. So long as this faith remains inviolate and firm, we may without blame entertain doubts regarding some things which we have neither perceived by sense nor by reason, and which have not been revealed to us by the canonical Scriptures, nor come to our knowledge through witnesses whom it is absurd to disbelieve.

In spite of the following chapter's title, its content is a very brief explanation of a Christian's duty to serve as Augustine did as a bishop to his diocese.

CHAPTER 19

OF THE DRESS AND HABITS OF THE CHRISTIAN PEOPLE

It is a matter of no moment in the city of God whether he who adopts the faith that brings men to God adopts it in one dress and manner of life or another, so long only as he lives in conformity with the commandments of God. And hence, when philosophers themselves become Christians, they are compelled, indeed, to abandon their erroneous doctrines, but not their dress and mode of living, which are no obstacle to religion. So that we make no account of that distinction of sects which Varro adduced in connection with the Cynic school, provided always nothing indecent or self-indulgent is retained. As to these three modes of life, the contemplative, the active, and the composite, although, so long as a man's faith is preserved, he may choose any of them without detriment to his eternal interests, yet he must never overlook the claims of truth and duty. No man has a right to lead such a life of contemplation as to forget in his own ease the service due to his neighbor; nor has any man a right to be so immersed in active life as to neglect the contemplation of God. The charm of leisure must not be indolent vacancy of mind, but the investigation or discovery of truth, that thus every man may make solid attainments without grudging that others do the same. And, in active life, it is not the honors or power of this life we should covet, since all things under the sun are vanity, but we should aim at using our position and influence, if these have been honorably attained, for the welfare of those who are under us, in the way we have already explained. It is to this the apostle refers when he says, "He that desireth the episcopate desireth a good work." He wished to show that the episcopate is the title of a work, not of an honor. It is a Greek word, and signifies that he who governs superintends or takes care of those whom he governs: for ἐπί means over, and σκοπεῖν, to see; therefore ἐπισκοπεῖν means "to oversee." So that he who loves to govern rather than to do good is no bishop. Accordingly no one is prohibited from the search after truth, for in this leisure may most laudably be spent; but it is unseemly to covet the high position requisite for governing the people, even though that position be held and that government be administered in a seemly manner. And therefore holy leisure is longed for by the love of truth; but it is the necessity of love to undertake requisite business. If no one imposes this burden upon us, we are free to sift and contemplate truth; but if it be laid upon us, we are necessitated for love's sake to undertake it. And yet not even in this case are we obliged wholly to relinquish the sweets of contemplation; for were these to be withdrawn, the burden might prove more than we could bear.

CHAPTER 20

THAT THE SAINTS ARE IN THIS LIFE BLESSED IN HOPE

Since, then, the supreme good of the city of God is perfect and eternal peace, not such as mortals pass into and out of by birth and death, but the peace of freedom from all evil, in which the immortals ever abide, who can deny that that future life is most blessed, or that, in comparison with it, this life which now we live is most wretched, be it filled with all blessings of body and soul and external things? And yet, if any man uses this life with a reference to that other which he ardently loves and confidently hopes for, he may well be called even now blessed, though not in reality so much as in hope. But the actual possession of the happiness of this life, without the hope of what is beyond, is but a false happiness and profound misery. For the true blessings of the soul are not now enjoyed; for that is no true wisdom which does not direct all its prudent observations, manly actions, virtuous self-restraint, and just arrangements, to that end in which God shall be all and all in a secure eternity and perfect peace.

CHAPTER 21

WHETHER THERE EVER WAS A ROMAN REPUBLIC
ANSWERING TO THE DEFINITIONS OF SCIPIO
IN CICERO'S DIALOGUE

This, then, is the place where I should fulfill the promise given in the second book of this work, and explain, as briefly and clearly as possible, that if we are to accept the definitions laid down by Scipio in Cicero's *De Republica*, there never was a Roman republic; for he briefly defines a republic as the weal of the people. And if this definition be true, there never was a Roman republic, for the people's weal was never attained among the

Romans. For the people, according to his definition, is an assemblage associated by a common acknowledgment of right and by a community of interests. And what he means by a common acknowledgment of right he explains at large, showing that a republic cannot be administered without justice. Where, therefore, there is no true justice there can be no right. For that which is done by right is justly done, and what is unjustly done cannot be done by right. For the unjust inventions of men are neither to be considered nor spoken of as rights; for even they themselves say that right is that which flows from the fountain of justice, and deny the definition which is commonly given by those who misconceive the matter, that right is that which is useful to the stronger party. Thus, where there is not true justice there can be no assemblage of men associated by a common acknowledgment of right, and therefore there can be no people, as defined by Scipio or Cicero; and if no people, then no weal of the people, but only of some promiscuous multitude unworthy of the name of people. Consequently, if the republic is the weal of the people, and there is no people if it be not associated by a common acknowledgment of right, and if there is no right where there is no justice, then most certainly it follows that there is no republic where there is no justice. Further, justice is that virtue which gives every one his due. Where, then, is the justice of man, when he deserts the true God and yields himself to impure demons? Is this to give every one his due? Or is he who keeps back a piece of ground from the purchaser, and gives it to a man who has no right to it, unjust, while he who keeps back himself from the God who made him, and serves wicked spirits, is just?

This same book, *De Republica*, advocates the cause of justice against injustice with great force and keenness. The pleading for injustice against justice was first heard, and it was asserted that without injustice a republic could neither increase nor even subsist, for it was laid down as an absolutely unassailable position that it is unjust for some men to rule and some to serve; and yet the imperial city to which the republic belongs cannot rule her provinces without having recourse to this injustice. It was replied in behalf of justice, that this ruling of the provinces is just, because servitude may be advantageous to the provincials, and is so when rightly administered—that is to say, when lawless men are prevented from doing harm. And further, as they became worse and worse so long as they were free, they will improve by subjection. To confirm this reasoning, there is added an eminent example drawn from nature: for "why," it is asked, "does God rule man, the soul the body, the reason the passions and other vicious parts of the soul?" This example leaves no doubt that, to some, servitude is useful; and, indeed, to serve God is useful to all. And it is when the soul serves God that it exercises a right control over the body; and in the soul itself the reason must be subject to God if it is to govern as it ought the passions and other vices. Hence, when a man does not serve God, what justice can we ascribe to him, since in this case his soul cannot exercise a just control over the body, nor his reason over his vices? And if there is no justice in such an individual, certainly there can be none in a community composed of such persons. Here, therefore, there is not that common acknowledgment of right which makes an assemblage of men a people whose affairs we call a republic. And why need I speak of the advantageousness, the common participation in which, according to the definition, makes a people? For although, if you choose to regard the matter attentively, you will see that there is nothing advantageous to those who live godlessly, as every one lives who does not serve God but demons, whose wickedness you may measure by their desire to receive the worship of men though they are most impure spirits, yet what I have said of the common acknowledgment of right is enough to demonstrate that, according to the above definition, there can be no people, and therefore no republic, where there is no justice. For if they assert that in their republic the Romans did not serve unclean spirits, but good and holy gods, must we therefore again reply to this evasion, though already we have said enough, and more than enough, to expose it? He must be an uncommonly stupid, or a shamelessly contentious person, who has read through the foregoing books to this point, and can yet question whether the Romans served wicked and impure demons. But, not to speak of their character, it is written in the law of the true God, "He that sacrificeth unto any god save unto the Lord only, he shall be utterly destroyed." He, therefore, who uttered so menacing a commandment decreed that no worship should be given either to good or bad gods.

CHAPTER 22

WHETHER THE GOD WHOM THE CHRISTIANS
SERVE IS THE TRUE GOD TO WHOM ALONE
SACRIFICE OUGHT TO BE PAID

But it may be replied, Who is this God, or what proof is there that He alone is worthy to receive sacrifice from the Romans? One must be very blind to be still asking who this God is. He is the God whose prophets predicted the things we see accomplished. He is the God from whom Abraham received the assurance, "In thy seed shall all nations be blessed." That this was fulfilled in Christ, who according to the flesh sprang from that seed, is recognized, whether they will or no, even by those who have continued to be the enemies of this name. He is the God whose divine Spirit spake by the men whose predictions I cited in the preceding books, and which are fulfilled in the Church which has extended over all the world. This is the God whom Varro, the most learned of the Romans, supposed to be Jupiter, though he knows not what he says; yet I think it right to note the circumstance that a man of such learning was unable to suppose that this God had no existence or was contemptible, but believed Him to be the same as the supreme God. In fine, He is the God whom Porphyry, the most learned of the philosophers, though the bitterest enemy of the Christians, confesses to be a great God, even according to the oracles of those whom he esteems gods.

In chapter 23, after a long discussion of Porphyry's attack on Christianity (by no means the only one), Augustine returns to the question whether an earthly republic can be a true republic, and concludes that strictly speaking it is very likely, and in the case of a pagan state, it is certain, that it cannot.

CHAPTER 23

PORPHYRY'S ACCOUNT OF THE RESPONSES GIVEN BY
THE ORACLES OF THE GODS CONCERNING CHRIST

. . . where there is not this righteousness whereby the one supreme God rules the obedient city according to His grace, so that it sacrifices to none but Him, and whereby, in all the citizens of this obedient city, the soul consequently rules the body and reason the vices in the rightful order, so that, as the individual just man, so also the community and people of the just, live by faith, which works by love, that love whereby man loves God as He ought to be loved, and his neighbor as himself—there, I say, there is not an assemblage associated by a common acknowledgment of right, and by a community of interests. But if there is not this, there is not a people, if our definition be true, and therefore there is no republic; for where there is no people there can be no republic.

CHAPTER 24

THE DEFINITION WHICH MUST BE GIVEN OF
A PEOPLE AND A REPUBLIC, IN ORDER TO VINDICATE
THE ASSUMPTION OF THESE TITLES BY THE ROMANS
AND BY OTHER KINGDOMS

But if we discard this definition of a people, and, assuming another, say that a people is an assemblage of reasonable beings bound together by a common agreement as to the objects of their love, then, in order to discover the character of any people, we have only to observe what they love. Yet whatever it loves, if only it is an assemblage of reasonable beings and not of beasts, and is bound together by an agreement as to the objects of love, it is reasonably called a people; and

it will be a superior people in proportion as it is
bound together by higher interests, inferior in proportion as it is bound together by lower. According
to this definition of ours, the Roman people is a
people, and its weal is without doubt a commonwealth or republic. But what its tastes were in its
early and subsequent days, and how it declined into
sanguinary seditions and then to social and civil
wars, and so burst asunder or rotted off the bond of
concord in which the health of a people consists, history shows, and in the preceding books I have related
at large. And yet I would not on this account say
either that it was not a people, or that its administration was not a republic, so long as there remains an
assemblage of reasonable beings bound together by a
common agreement as to the objects of love. But
what I say of this people and of this republic I must
be understood to think and say of the Athenians or
any Greek state, of the Egyptians, of the early Assyr-
ian Babylon, and of every other nation, great or small,
which had a public government. For, in general, the
city of the ungodly, which did not obey the command of God that it should offer no sacrifice save to
Him alone, and which, therefore, could not give to the
soul its proper command over the body, nor to the reason its just authority over the vices, is void of true
justice.

CHAPTER 25

THAT WHERE THERE IS NO TRUE RELIGION
THERE ARE NO TRUE VIRTUES

For though the soul may seem to rule the body admirably, and the reason the vices, if the soul and reason do not themselves obey God, as God has commanded them to serve Him, they have no proper authority over the body and the vices. For what kind of mistress of the body and the vices can that mind be which is ignorant of the true God, and which, instead of being subject to His authority, is prostituted to the corrupting influences of the most vicious demons? It is for this reason that the virtues which it seems to itself to possess, and by which it restrains the body and the vices that it may obtain and keep what it desires, are rather vices than virtues so long as there is no reference to God in the matter. For although some suppose that virtues which have a reference only to themselves, and are desired only on their own account, are yet true and genuine virtues, the fact is that even then they are inflated with pride, and are therefore to be reckoned vices rather than virtues. For as that which gives life to the flesh is not derived from flesh, but is above it, so that which gives blessed life to man is not derived from man, but is something above him; and what I say of man is true of every celestial power and virtue whatsoever.

CHAPTER 26

OF THE PEACE WHICH IS ENJOYED BY THE PEOPLE THAT

ARE ALIENATED FROM GOD, AND THE USE MADE OF IT BY

THE PEOPLE OF GOD IN THE TIME OF ITS PILGRIMAGE

Wherefore, as the life of the flesh is the soul, so the blessed life of man is God, of whom the sacred writings of the Hebrews say, "Blessed is the people whose God is the Lord." Miserable, therefore, is the people which is alienated from God. Yet even this people has a peace of its own which is not to be lightly esteemed, though, indeed, it shall not in the end enjoy it, because it makes no good use of it before the end. But it is our interest that it enjoy this peace meanwhile in this life; for as long as the two cities are commingled, we also enjoy the peace of Babylon. For from Babylon the people of God is so freed that it meanwhile sojourns in its company. And therefore the apostle also admonished the Church to pray for kings and those in authority, assigning as the reason, "that we may live a quiet and tranquil life in all godliness and love." And the prophet Jeremiah, when predicting the captivity that was to befall the ancient people of God, and giving them the divine command to go obediently to Babylonia, and thus serve their God, counselled them also to pray for Babylonia, saying, "In the peace thereof shall ye have peace"—the temporal peace which the good and the wicked together enjoy.

CHAPTER 27

THAT THE PEACE OF THOSE WHO SERVE GOD
CANNOT IN THIS MORTAL LIFE BE APPREHENDED
IN ITS PERFECTION

But the peace which is peculiar to ourselves we enjoy now with God by faith, and shall hereafter enjoy eternally with Him by sight. But the peace which we enjoy in this life, whether common to all or peculiar to ourselves, is rather the solace of our misery than the positive enjoyment of felicity. Our very righteousness, too, though true in so far as it has respect to the true good, is yet in this life of such a kind that it consists rather in the remission of sins than in the perfecting of virtues. Witness the prayer of the whole city of God in its pilgrim state, for it cries to God by the mouth of all its members, "Forgive us our debts as we forgive our debtors." And this prayer is efficacious not for those whose faith is "without works and dead," but for those whose faith "worketh by love." For as reason, though subjected to God, is yet "pressed down by the corruptible body," so long as it is in this mortal condition, it has not perfect authority over vice, and therefore this prayer is needed by the righteous. For though it exercises authority, the vices do not submit without a struggle. For however well one maintains the conflict, and however thoroughly he has subdued these enemies, there steals in some evil thing, which, if it do not find ready expression in act, slips out by the lips, or insinuates itself into the thought; and therefore his peace is not full so long as he is at war with his vices. For it is a doubtful conflict he wages with those that resist, and his victory over those that are defeated is not secure, but full of anxiety and effort. Amidst these temptations, therefore, of all which it has been summarily said in the divine oracles, "Is not human life upon earth a temptation?" who but a proud man can presume that he so lives that he has no need to say to God, "Forgive us our debts?" And such a man is not great, but swollen and puffed up with vanity, and is justly resisted by Him who abundantly gives grace to the humble. Whence it is said, "God resisteth the proud, but giveth grace to the humble." In this, then, consists the righteousness of a man, that he submit himself to God, his body to his soul, and his vices, even when they rebel, to his reason, which either defeats or at least resists them; and also that he beg from God grace to do his duty, and the pardon of his sins, and that he render to God thanks for all the blessings he receives. But, in that final peace to which all our righteousness has reference, and for the sake of which it is maintained, as our nature shall enjoy a sound immortality and incorruption, and shall have no more vices, and as we shall experience no resistance either from ourselves or from others, it will not be necessary that reason should rule vices which no longer exist, but God shall rule the man, and the soul shall rule the body, with a sweetness and facility suitable to the felicity of a life which is done with bondage. And this condition shall there be eternal, and we shall be assured of its eternity; and thus the peace of this blessedness and the blessedness of this peace shall be the supreme good.

CHAPTER 28

THE END OF THE WICKED

But, on the other hand, they who do not belong to this city of God shall inherit eternal misery, which is also called the second death, because the soul shall then be separated from God its life, and therefore cannot be said to live, and the body shall be subjected to eternal pains. And consequently this second death shall be the more severe, because no death shall terminate it. But war being contrary to peace, as misery to happiness, and life to death, it is not without reason asked what kind of war can be found in the end of the wicked answering to the peace which is declared to be the end of the righteous? The person who puts this question has only to observe what it is in war that is hurtful and destructive, and he shall see that it is nothing else than the mutual opposition and conflict of things. And can he conceive a more grievous and bitter war than that in which the will is so opposed to passion, and passion to the will, that their hostility can never be terminated by the victory of either, and in which the violence of pain so conflicts with the nature of the body, that neither yields to the other? For in this life, when this conflict has arisen, either pain conquers and death expels the feeling of it, or nature conquers and health expels the pain. But in the world to come the pain continues that it may torment, and the nature endures that it may be sensible of it; and neither ceases to exist, lest punishment also should cease. Now, as it is through the last judgment that men pass to these ends, the good to the supreme good, the evil to the supreme evil, I will treat of this judgment in the following book.

CONTRA FAUSTUM

An example of Augustine's polemical style is his tract Contra Faustum, *written around 400, and addressed to the views of a Manichaean "bishop," Faustus. He had raised, among other issues, the difficulty of reconciling Christ's injunctions to turn the other cheek with the violence of the Old Testament and present-day military and judicial violence.*

70. It might be shown that, though Moses slew the Egyptian, without being commanded by God, the

action was divinely permitted, as, from the prophetic character of Moses, it prefigured something in the future. Now however, I do not use this argument, but view the action as having no symbolical meaning. In the light, then, of the eternal law, it was wrong for one who had no legal authority to kill the man, even though he was a bad character, besides being the aggressor. But in minds where great virtue is to come, there is often an early crop of vices, in which we may still discern a disposition for some particular virtue, which will come when the mind is duly cultivated. For as farmers, when they see land bringing forth huge crops, though of weeds, pronounce it good for corn; or when they see wild creepers, which have to be rooted out, still consider the land good for useful vines; and when they see a hill covered with wild olives, conclude that with culture it will produce good fruit: so the disposition of mind which led Moses to take the law into his own hands, to prevent the wrong done to his brother, living among strangers, by a wicked citizen of the country from being unrequited, was not unfit for the production of virtue, but from want of culture gave signs of its productiveness in an unjustifiable manner. He who afterwards, by His angel, called Moses on Mount Sinai, with the divine commission to liberate the people of Israel from Egypt, and who trained him to obedience by the miraculous appearance in the bush burning but not consumed, and by instructing him in his ministry, was the same who, by the call addressed from heaven to Saul when persecuting the Church, humbled him, raised him up, and animated him; or in figurative words, by this stroke He cut off the branch, grafted it, and made it fruitful. For the fierce energy of Paul, when in his zeal for hereditary traditions he persecuted the Church, thinking that he was doing God service, was like a crop of weeds showing great signs of productiveness. It was the same in Peter, when he took his sword out of its sheath to defend the Lord, and cut off the right ear of an assailant, when the Lord rebuked him with something like a threat, saying, "Put up thy sword into its sheath; for he that taketh the sword shall perish by the sword." To take the sword is to use weapons against a man's life, without the sanction of the constituted authority. The Lord, indeed, had told His disciples to carry a sword; but He did not tell them to use it. But that after this sin Peter should become a pastor of the Church was no more improper than that Moses, after smiting the Egyptian, should become the leader of the congregation. In both cases the trespass originated not in inveterate cruelty, but in a hasty zeal which admitted of correction. In both cases there was resentment against injury, accompanied in one case by love for a brother, and in the other by love, though still carnal, of the Lord. Here was evil to be subdued or rooted out; but the heart with such capacities needed only, like good soil, to be cultivated to make it fruitful in virtue.

71. Then, as for Faustus' objection to the spoiling of the Egyptians, he knows not what he says. In this Moses not only did not sin, but it would have been sin not to do it. It was by the command of God, who, from His knowledge both of the actions and of the hearts of men, can decide on what every one should be made to suffer, and through whose agency. The people at that time were still carnal, and engrossed with earthly affections; while the Egyptians were in open rebellion against God, for they used the gold, God's creature, in the service of idols, to the dishonor of the Creator, and they had grievously oppressed strangers by making them work without pay. Thus the Egyptians deserved the punishment, and the Israelites were suitably employed in inflicting it. Perhaps, indeed, it was not so much a command as a permission to the Hebrews to act in the matter according to their own inclinations; and God, in sending the message by Moses, only wished that they should thus be informed of His permission. There may also have been mysterious reasons for what God said to the people on this matter. At any rate, God's commands are to be submissively received, not to be argued against. The apostle says, "Who hath known the mind of the Lord? or who hath been His counsellor?" Whether, then, the reason was what I have said, or

whether in the secret appointment of God, there was some unknown reason for His telling the people by Moses to borrow things from the Egyptians, and to take them away with them, this remains certain, that this was said for some good reason, and that Moses could not lawfully have done otherwise than God told him, leaving to God the reason of the command, while the servant's duty is to obey.

72. But, says Faustus, it cannot be admitted that the true God, who is also good, ever gave such a command. I answer, such a command can be rightly given by no other than the true and good God, who alone knows the suitable command in every case, and who alone is incapable of inflicting unmerited suffering on any one. This ignorant and spurious goodness of the human heart may as well deny what Christ says, and object to the wicked being made to suffer by the good God, when He shall say to the angels, "Gather first the tares into bundles to burn them." The servants, however, were stopped when they wished to do this prematurely: "Lest by chance, when ye would gather the tares, ye root up the wheat also with them." Thus the true and good God alone knows when, to whom, and by whom to order anything, or to permit anything. In the same way, this human goodness, or folly rather, might object to the Lord's permitting the devils to enter the swine, which they asked to be allowed to do with a

mischievous intent? especially as the Manichaeans believe that not only pigs, but the vilest insects, have human souls. But setting aside these absurd notions, this is undeniable, that our Lord Jesus Christ, the only son of God, and therefore the true and good God, permitted the destruction of swine belonging to strangers, implying loss of life and of a great amount of property, at the request of devils. No one can be so insane as to suppose that Christ could not have driven the devils out of the men without gratifying their malice by the destruction of the swine. If, then, the Creator and Governor of all natures, in His superintendence, which, though mysterious, is ever just, indulged the violent and unjust inclination of those lost spirits already doomed to eternal fire, why should not the Egyptians, who were unrighteous oppressors, be spoiled by the Hebrews, a free people, who would claim payment for their enforced and painful toil, especially as the earthly possessions which they thus lost were used by the Egyptians in their impious rites, to the dishonor of the Creator? Still, if Moses had originated this order, or if the people had done it spontaneously, undoubtedly it would have been sinful; and perhaps the people did sin, not in doing what God commanded or permitted, but in some desire of their own for what they took. The permission given to this action by divine authority was in accordance with the just and good counsel of Him who uses punishments both to restrain the wicked and to educate His own people; who knows also how to give more advanced precepts to those able to bear them, while He begins on a lower scale in the treatment of the feeble. As for Moses, he can be blamed neither for coveting the property, nor for disputing, in any instance, the divine authority.

73. According to the eternal law, which requires the preservation of natural order, and forbids the transgression of it, some actions have an indifferent character, so that men are blamed for presumption if they do them without being called upon, while they are deservedly praised for doing them when required. The act, the agent, and the authority for the action are all of great importance in the order of nature. For Abraham to sacrifice his son of his own accord is shocking madness. His doing so at the command of God proves him faithful and submissive. This is so loudly proclaimed by the very voice of truth, that Faustus, eagerly rummaging for some fault, and reduced at last to slanderous charges, has not the boldness to attack this action. It is scarcely possible that he can have forgotten a deed so famous, that it recurs to the mind of itself without any study or reflection, and is in fact repeated by so many tongues, and portrayed in so many places, that no one can pretend to shut his eyes or his ears to it. If, therefore, while Abraham's killing his son of his own accord would have

been unnatural, his doing it at the command of God shows not only guiltless but praiseworthy compliance, why does Faustus blame Moses for spoiling the Egyptians? Your feeling of disapproval for the mere human action should be restrained by a regard for the divine sanction. Will you venture to blame God Himself for desiring such actions? Then "Get thee behind me, Satan, for thou understandest not the things which be of God, but those which be of men." Would that this rebuke might accomplish in you what it did in Peter, and that you might hereafter preach the truth concerning God, which you now, judging by feeble sense, find fault with! as Peter became a zealous messenger to announce to the Gentiles what he objected to at first, when the Lord spoke of it as His intention.

74. Now, if this explanation suffices to satisfy human obstinacy and perverse misinterpretation of right actions of the vast difference between the indulgence of passion and presumption on the part of men, and obedience to the command of God, who knows what to permit or to order, and also the time and the persons, and the due action or suffering in each case, the account of the wars of Moses will not excite surprise or abhorrence, for in wars carried on by divine command, he showed not ferocity but obedience; and God in giving the command, acted not in cruelty, but in righteous retribution, giving to all what they deserved, and warn-

ing those who needed warning. What is the evil in war? Is it the death of some who will soon die in any case, that others may live in peaceful subjection? This is mere cowardly dislike, not any religious feeling. The real evils in war are love of violence, revengeful cruelty, fierce and implacable enmity, wild resistance, and the lust of power, and such like; and it is generally to punish these things, when force is required to inflict the punishment, that, in obedience to God or some lawful authority, good men undertake wars, when they find themselves in such a position as regards the conduct of human affairs, that right conduct requires them to act, or to make others act in this way. Otherwise John, when the soldiers who came to be baptized asked, What shall we do? would have replied, Throw away your arms; give up the service; never strike, or wound, or disable any one. But knowing that such actions in battle were not murderous but authorized by law, and that the soldiers did not thus avenge themselves, but defend the public safety, he replied, "Do violence to no man, accuse no man falsely, and be content with your wages." But as the Manichaeans are in the habit of speaking evil of John, let them hear the Lord Jesus Christ Himself ordering this money to be given to Caesar, which John tells the soldiers to be content with. "Give," He says, "to Caesar the things that are Caesar's." For tribute-money is given on purpose to pay the soldiers for war. Again, in the case of the centurion who said, "I am a man under authority, and have soldiers under me: and I say to one, Go, and he goeth; and to another, Come, and he cometh; and to my servant, Do this, and he doeth it," Christ gave due praise to his faith; He did not tell him to leave the service. But there is no need here to enter on the long discussion of just and unjust ways.

75. A great deal depends on the causes for which men undertake wars, and on the authority they have for doing so; for the natural order which seeks the peace of mankind, ordains that the monarch should have the power of undertaking war if he thinks it advisable, and that the soldiers should perform their military duties in behalf of the peace and safety of the community. When war is undertaken in obedience to God, who would rebuke, or humble, or crush the pride of man, it must be allowed to be a righteous war; for even the wars which arise from human passion cannot harm the eternal well-being of God, nor even hurt His saints; for in the trial of their patience, and the chastening of their spirit, and in bearing fatherly correction, they are rather benefited than injured. No one can have any power against them but what is given him from above. For there is no power but of God, who either orders or permits. Since, therefore, a righteous man, serving it may be under an ungodly king, may do the duty belonging to his position in the State in fighting by the order of his sover-

eign—for in some cases it is plainly the will of God that he should fight, and in others, where this is not so plain, it may be an unrighteous command on the part of the king, while the soldier is innocent, because his position makes obedience a duty—how much more must the man be blameless who carries on war on the authority of God, of whom every one who serves Him knows that He can never require what is wrong?

76. If it is supposed that God could not enjoin warfare, because in after times it was said by the Lord Jesus Christ, "I say unto you, That ye resist not evil: but if any one strike thee on the right cheek, turn to him the left also," the answer is, that what is here required is not a bodily action, but an inward disposition. The sacred seat of virtue is the heart, and such were the hearts of our fathers, the righteous men of old. But order required such a regulation of events, and such a distinction of times, as to show first of all that even earthly blessings (for so temporal kingdoms and victory over enemies are considered to be, and these are the things which the community of the ungodly all over the world are continually begging from idols and devils) are entirely under the control and at the disposal of the one true God. Thus, under the Old Testament, the secret of the kingdom of heaven, which was to be disclosed in due time, was veiled, and so far obscured, in the disguise of earthly promises. But when the fullness of time came

for the revelation of the New Testament, which was hidden under the types of the Old, clear testimony was to be borne to the truth, that there is another life for which this life ought to be disregarded, and another kingdom for which the opposition of all earthly kingdoms should be patiently borne. Thus the name martyrs, which means witnesses, was given to those who, by the will of God, bore this testimony, by their confessions, their sufferings, and their death. The number of such witnesses is so great, that if it pleased Christ—who called Saul by a voice from heaven, and having changed him from a wolf to a sheep, sent him into the midst of wolves—to unite them all in one army, and to give them success in battle, as He gave to the Hebrews, what nation could withstand them? what kingdom would remain unsubdued? But as the doctrine of the New Testament is, that we must serve God not for temporal happiness in this life, but for eternal felicity hereafter, this truth was most strikingly confirmed by the patient endurance of what is commonly called adversity for the sake of that felicity. So in fullness of time the Son of God, made of a woman, made under the law, that He might redeem them that were under the law, made of the seed of David according to the flesh sends His disciples as sheep into the midst of wolves, and bids them not fear those that can kill the body, but cannot kill the soul, and promises that even the body will be entirely restored, so that not a hair shall be lost. Peter's sword He orders back into its sheath, restoring as it was before the ear of His enemy that had been cut off. He says that He could obtain legions of angels to destroy His enemies, but that He must drink the cup which His Father's will had given Him. He sets the example of drinking this cup, then hands it to His followers, manifesting thus, both in word and deed, the grace of patience. Therefore God raised Him from the dead, and has given Him a name which is above every name; that in the name of Jesus every knee should bow, of things in heaven and of things in earth, and of things under the earth; and that every tongue should confess that Jesus is Lord, to the glory of God the Father. The patriarchs and prophets, then, have a kingdom in this world, to show that these kingdoms, too, are given and taken away by God: the apostles and martyrs had no kingdom here, to show the superior desirableness of the kingdom of heaven. The prophets, however, could even in those times die for the truth, as the Lord Himself says, "From the blood of Abel to the blood of Zacharia"; and in these days, since the commencement of the fulfillment of what is prophesied in the psalm of Christ, under the figure of Solomon, which means the peacemaker, as Christ is our peace, "All kings of the earth shall bow to Him, all nations shall serve Him," we have seen Christian emperors, who have put all their confidence in

Christ, gaining splendid victories over ungodly enemies, whose hope was in the rites of idolatry and devil-worship. There are public and undeniable proofs of the fact, that on one side the prognostications of devils were found to be fallacious, and on the other, the predictions of saints were a means of support; and we have now writings in which those facts are recorded. . . .

79. Let no one, then, be so daring as to make rash charges against men, not to say against God. If the service of the ministers of the Old Testament, who were also heralds of the New, consisted in putting sinners to death, and that of the ministers of the New Testament, who are also interpreters of the Old, in being put to death by sinners, the service in both cases is rendered to one God, who, varying the lesson to suit the times, teaches both that temporal blessings are to be sought from Him, and that they are to be forsaken for Him, and that temporal distress is both sent by Him and should be endured for Him. There was, therefore, no cruelty in the command, or in the action of Moses, when, in his holy jealousy for his people, whom he wished to be subject to the one true God, on learning that they had fallen away to the worship of an idol made by their own hands, he impressed their minds at the time with a wholesome fear, and gave them a warning for the future, by using the sword in the punishment of a few, whose just punishment God, against whom they

had sinned, appointed in the depth of His secret judgment to be immediately inflicted. That Moses acted as
he did, not in cruelty, but in great love, may be seen
from the words in which he prayed for the sins of the
people: "If Thou wilt forgive their sin, forgive it; and if
not, blot me out of Thy book." The pious inquirer who
compares the slaughter with the prayer will find in this
the clearest evidence of the awful nature of the injury
done to the soul by prostitution to the images of devils,
since such love is roused to such anger. We see the same
in the apostle, who, not in cruelty, but in love, delivered
a man up to Satan for the destruction of the flesh, that
the spirit might be saved in the day of the Lord Jesus.
Others, too, he delivered up, that they might learn not
to blaspheme. In the apocryphal books of the Manichaeans there is a collection of fables, published by
some unknown authors under the name of the apostles.
The books would no doubt have been sanctioned by the
Church at the time of their publication, if holy and
learned men then in life, and competent to determine
the matter, had thought the contents to be true. One of
the stories is, that the Apostle Thomas was once at a
marriage feast in a country where he was unknown,
when one of the servants struck him, and that he forthwith by his curse brought a terrible punishment on this
man. For when he went out to the fountain to provide
water for the guests, a lion fell on him and killed him,

and the hand with which he had given a slight blow to the apostle was torn off, in fulfillment of the imprecation, and brought by a dog to the table at which the apostle was reclining. What could be more cruel than this? And yet, if I mistake not, the story goes on to say, that the apostle made up for the cruelty by obtaining for the man the blessing of pardon in the next world; so that, while the people of this strange country learned to fear the apostle as being so dear to God, the man's eternal welfare was secured in exchange for the loss of this mortal life. It matters not whether the story is true or false. At any rate, the Manichaeans, who regard as genuine and authentic books which the canon of the Church rejects, must allow, as shown in the story, that the virtue of patience, which the Lord enjoins when He says, "If any one smite thee on the right cheek, turn to him thy left also," may be in the inward disposition, though it is not exhibited in bodily action or in words. For when the apostle was struck, instead of turning his other side to the man, or telling him to repeat the blow, he prayed to God to pardon his assailant in the next world, but not to leave the injury unpunished at the time. Inwardly he preserved a kindly feeling, while outwardly he wished the man to be punished as an example. As the Manichaeans believe this, rightly or wrongly, they may also believe that such was the intention of Moses, the servant of God, when he cut down with the sword the makers and worshippers of the idol; for his own words show that he so entreated for pardon for their sin of idolatry as to ask to be blotted out of God's book if his prayer was not heard. There is no comparison between a stranger being struck with the hand, and the dishonor done to God by forsaking Him for an idol, when He had brought the people out of the bondage of Egypt, had led them through the sea, and had covered with the waters the enemy pursuing them. Nor, as regards the punishment, is there any comparison between being killed with the sword and being torn in pieces by wild beasts. For judges in administering the law condemn to exposure to wild beasts worse criminals than are condemned to be put to death by the sword.

ABOUT THE AUTHOR

Alan Ryan was born in London in 1940 and educated at Oxford University, where he taught for many years. He was professor of politics at Princeton University from 1988 to 1996, and warden of New College, Oxford University, and professor of political theory from 1996 until 2009. He is the author of *The Philosophy of John Stuart Mill*, *The Philosophy of the Social Sciences*, *J. S. Mill, Property and Political Theory*, *Bertrand Russell: A Political Life*, *John Dewey and the High Tide of American Liberalism*, *Liberal Anxieties and Liberal Education*, and *On Politics*. He is married to Kate Ryan.